LI̸
HO

G000161944

The Author

For over twenty years, Corkwoman Mary Lynch has been known to many people as Liz Kavanagh. *Country Living*, the first volume of her collected writings from *The Irish Farmers' Journal*, was published in 1997. Just before its publication, Mary was involved in an accident. Instead of attending the launch of her book, she found herself in a hospital bed, with a broken back. Nevertheless, the book went on to become a great success, and its author is making a remarkable recovery. The many months she spent in bed provided her with much time to reflect on past years and to bring together more of her *Farmers' Journal* writings for *Home to Roost*.

*I dedicate this book to
my long-suffering daughters-in-law
and their husbands*

U. ejahan
Christmas 98

LIZ KAVANAGH
HOME TO ROOST

WOLFHOUND PRESS

First published in 1998 by
Wolfhound Press Ltd
68 Mountjoy Square
Dublin 1, Ireland
Tel: (353-1) 874 0354
Fax: (353-1) 872 0207

The Arts Council
An Chomhairle Ealaíon
Wolfhound Press receives financial assistance from The Arts Council/An Chomhairle Ealaíon, Dublin, Ireland.

British Library Cataloguing in Publication Data
A catalogue record for this book is available from the British Library.

ISBN 0-86327-686-5

10 9 8 7 6 5 4 3 2 1

Cover Photograph: Slide File
Cover Design: Slick Fish Design
Typesetting: Wolfhound Press
Printed in the Republic of Ireland by Colour Books, Dublin.

Contents

PREFACE

'What's Another Year?' won the Eurovision song contest the year I was on the Irish Eurovision jury. 'What indeed?' most of us may say as year follows on year with little to mark them apart. We can all reel off some years immediately — the year we were born, did major exams, got married, had our children, were bereaved, and so on and so forth. Some years are remembered because of great joy, others for their sadness. Your special year will not be mine. I am hard pushed to remember the year any of my children got married. And I can hardly remember how old my grandchildren are, not to mind the actual date itself.

I do remember that year of the Eurovision, however, not only because of the excitement of all that, but because a few short months later, my son Seamus left home for good, the first fledging gone from the nest. He was gone, at seventeen, with just a note left for us on the breakfast table when we got up.

Another date unlikely to slip my mind for the rest of my of life is 17 September 1997. That was the day when, in my beloved garden, I overreached while on top of an extended ladder, fell fifteen feet onto concrete and broke my back. Eoin has often said that my garden would be the death of me. How nearly prophetic his words now seem even if they were never meant literally.

My mother, God rest her, hated us to comment on things going well. She probably never heard of the word hubris, that one fatal flaw of the protagonist in ancient Greek tragedies, which drew the anger of their gods down upon them. But she really hated any of us to say that things were going well, because she was convinced that things would then surely go wrong as a result.

The year 1997 will always be known as the year of my accident from now on. I've had other accidents in my life: Farming and accidents unfortunately seem to go hand in hand. But that one now qualifies as *the* accident, the one that put paid to some of my dreams for the future.

I had such a busy time planned for the latter part of 1997. There wasn't going to be time for me to draw breath, not to mind think. My MA thesis neared completion by its due date. *Country Living*, my first book, was due out with a grand launch, and I sure intended to suck every bit of enjoyment possible out of the planned publicity trail to boost sales, up until Christmas. Then, for when all that was done, Eoin and I had arranged the trip of a lifetime, visiting family all over the world, as we circumnavigated the globe.

Instead the family came to visit me. My chickens all came home to roost. And, instead of having no time to think, I finished up with much too much time to think. Down, but not out, would best describe me, both physically and mentally, in the aftermath of my accident. And, as always, my weekly column in the *Farmers' Journal* became a vehicle for both the release of pain and the sharing of joy and expectations. This column also brought me great comfort in a tough period of my life, as so many of you took the time out to write to me, to cheer me up and to tell me how you prayed for me.

I have a great advantage in that, now, unable to do much else, I can read the back issues of the *Farmers' Journal*, as well as all my original copies, parts of which never got beyond the editor's eagle eye. Thus I am reminded of events that had long slipped my mind. Some made me laugh, while others made me sad — nostalgic even — for times that are gone. However, with the benefit of hindsight, I can now quite clearly see my fatal touch of hubris.

I was determined, from a very early age, to be different,

to go my way regardless. I knew that I was not going to make the same stupid mistakes as others when my turn came. Now much older, if not wiser, I see that I did make similar mistakes. My expectations and plans did not always work out and, at times, I found my chickens coming home to roost in not quite the way I had expected. This started, when I was but nine years old, that Stephen's Day I went out as a wren-boy, purely for the money.

In all the years in between, the zip for my lip was not always kept as tightly shut as it could have been, especially when it came to sons and daughters-in-law. My beloved Eoin, however, as he once remarked, had already forgiven me my transgressions even before I committed them. Without him, I would have starved, physically and emotionally, this past year, as you will gather when you read on....

You will also see where, occasionally, I have added a postscript to some of the original articles, explaining just how those blessed chickens did indeed come home to roost on me! Some others have yet to land, I strongly suspect. I was not always, by today's standards, politically correct in my use of language. I wonder what my grandchildren, both born and unborn, will think of their grandmother and what she had to say for herself.

THE ACCIDENT

Getting Back on My Feet

I did it. I really did it. Today I walked. With Eoin holding me by the elbows, I got to a standing position by the bed and then took a couple of steps. The legs worked. They actually worked. I cannot begin to tell you what that meant to me since I cannot feel my left leg at all and my right leg isn't all that much better.

Then, while I was still on my feet, I suggested to him that we head for the door and back. Eoin reluctantly reversed and I advanced in a slow-motion shuffling sort of a dance, until we got there and back, and I happily collapsed on top of the bed, eyes closed, totally spent. Once he had me safely deposited, Eoin was on the phone, again and again, excitedly telling all our sons that their mother had walked. Next, for no reason I could see, he went out to the hospital corridor. He was back soon, however, rather crestfallen. He explained that he had found neither nurse nor doctor to whom he could impart the wonderful tidings. But he made up for that temporary setback by telling everyone who has come inside my door since. Finally, when he started to tell one nurse the same story for the third time, I had to tell him that everybody already knows. And she had only popped in to say goodbye since she was going on a different shift from tomorrow on.

Eoin and pain are the only two constants in my life these

past three weeks. I am now well into my fourth week in hospital, seeing only the faces that come near, but I have got very good at recognising people by voice and touch. Dozens of nurses have come and gone in that period. One big girl moves like an angel, her touch a benediction. But there is another wee lass whom I dread to hear approaching because she invariably bumps into the bed, both coming and going. And yet she is so kind, constantly checking if I am all right.

There is hope that my libido may be all right as well, despite the fact that I have no feeling whatsoever in the vaginal area. I say this because, for the first two weeks, I had the most gorgeous boy nurse tending to my needs. There are nine male nurses in his year, and plenty of male doctors and medical students — but this one would be at the very top of my shopping list if I was ever in the market for a toy-boy!

Then again, however, I would willingly have loved anyone once they came bearing syringes of pain relief, as my boy nurse did at regular intervals. I'd see that handsome young face, through the waves of pain, and know that soon I'd be floating disjointedly on a sea of drugs in which reality, mercifully, receded.

I still cannot think about the reality of that Wednesday morning with me on top of the ladder, overreaching and then falling, hopelessly clutching for anything to change the unchangeable. I still panic at the memory, breaking into a cold sweat as my mind skeeters like a spooked horse, away from that scene, to fasten on anything at all for distraction. So it may be some time, if ever, before I can talk about my stupidity, on top of the extended ladder, overreaching to clear a lump of grass, instead of coming down and letting Eoin move the ladder. He was holding it for safety. And, since I am the one with a head for heights, I was clearing out the year's debris from the gutters. Eoin had just said that he'd move the ladder when I said that I'd just get that lump of grass first.

Perhaps some day I may yet be grateful that I can

remember in such precise detail the fall, the pain, Eoin's panic and the endless wait for the ambulance with its hoped-for pain relief. Instead came increased agony, as, strapped down, I was moved onto the stretcher and into the vehicle while I begged for oblivion. Then we were off and my own screams came echoing back to me as I saw trees whiz by the windows. Finally, after what seemed an eternity on bumpy roads, I heard the traffic noises which heralded the outskirts of the city.

Eoin was not allowed into the ambulance with me. I was denied even that basic comfort. But he was there as the ambulance doors were opened and I was wheeled into the accident and emergency department. My sons were there too when I heard someone say that my back was badly broken, quite how badly they didn't know just yet. The grave voices all around me meant little to me now. At last, there was enough morphine in my system to help. Now too they had finally stopped moving me from place to place for an endless series of CAT scans and x-rays.

Through the impossible pain, and my screams at each movement, I had heard talk above me of an operation versus moving me to Dún Laoghaire. Somebody else said to wait and spoke of a styker bed where I could be both restrained and rotated while they awaited developments. There was talk too of the spinal cord being at least 70 per cent compromised. Terms like 'compromised' and talk of a 'styker bed' were only half heard and definitely not fully understood when all I wanted was yet another injection for the all-enveloping pain.

Thus began the past three weeks' nightmare, from which today I began to awake with those first steps of mine. I really feared I would never walk again. And, from the faces of my family, and their solicitude, I gather that so did they. They joy of a baby's first steps has nothing on the joy of walking for the second time around. And, like a baby, I can walk only if I am held upright.

As soon as I had recovered from my first exertion I tried a few steps once more. I didn't attempt the door the second time. But I shall, despite the fact that the doctors weren't too pleased when they heard of our success. Indeed, we were forbidden to repeat the exercise — 'There are physiotherapists here whose job that is.'

In all my time here, however, I have never seen sight nor sound of a physiotherapist. But Eoin is here all day and every day. And tomorrow, with his help, I intend not only to make the door, but also to get out on that corridor, since I haven't the faintest idea really of where I am.

Whistling at the Old Grey Mare

This should have been such a special week for us since Eoin and I will have been married forty years tomorrow. I had such plans and hopes for our ruby anniversary. Instead I am starting in on my fifth week in hospital, and nobody has talked to me about going home yet.

But I did have my sixth change of hospital bed during the week, and the nurse assured me that each change has been that bit nearer to the exit and away from under their eye. Each time I left behind the friends I had made and the comforting familiarity of the room and the routine I knew.

Now, as a VHI subscriber, I am at last, since yesterday, on the private floor of the regional hospital. So, after a few days, I will be able to state categorically the differences between public and private care. The most obvious so far is that I was Liz downstairs and I appear to have changed into Mrs Kavanagh up here. There is also a telephone and a television set here and gentle pink and green curtains. Downstairs the curtains were various shades of brown.

I just cannot understand the mentality of anyone who would choose brown curtains to surround sick people. I suspect some man or other must have decided that brown does not show the dirt.

I do not like the big mirror I have in my room here, over the hand-basin. When I was wheeled in here yesterday I saw myself for the first time in over four weeks. It was just like seeing a ghost of myself. White lips, white face, white roots — all were in horrible harmony. My hair hadn't even been washed, not to mind seeing a hairdresser for the duration. Then I noticed the punctured folds of flesh hanging grotesquely from my limbs.

I nearly had a relapse on the spot, and asked to be put back into bed before the legs gave way under me completely, which they threatened to do despite my walking frame. I am learning to walk again with that, and it is the greatest godsend. At least now I can go to the loo without looking for assistance. I spent weeks in nappies and with an ever-present catheter since my spinal injury robbed me of all control. Poor Eoin did things for me these past weeks that he never before had to do in all our forty years together.

When I was young, a test of true love among us girls was to imagine ourselves willingly using the loved one's toothbrush to wash our own teeth. Any involuntary shudder of revulsion meant that he was not yet the one true love. So, perhaps the test of his true love enduring is whether, as a husband of long or short standing, he would willingly, and without a shudder, change his wife's soiled nappy for her, washing her down where necessary, and then soothing the reddened flesh with talcum powder. I have had quite a bit of fun here in the bed, making lists of all the couples we know and deciding into which categories the husbands would fall. Oddly enough, we had no doubt whatsoever that all the wives would be both willing and able to do the needful.

Eoin has one unique skill, however, that I doubt any of the men we named would have. When my catheter was removed and I finally got to the loo, I found that neither gushing taps nor flowing showers were the slightest use. I

sat and sat but nothing happened. The nurses brought jugs
of water to flush me out. Then, even though I longed for
relief, nothing happened, even with jugs of water poured
between my legs. I just had no control over my lower body.

Leaving me still on the loo, the nurse said that she'd be
back to replace the catheter, a horrifying prospect. Yet the
only water that flowed from me were my tears, shed in a
mixture of fear and frustration, tingled with self-pity as
well, no doubt. Then Eoin — bless him — hovering over me,
suddenly remembered that, in his youth, his uncle always
whistled at mares in a special way to get them to urinate,
and so, standing guard at the bathroom door, he started in
on this persistent, monotonous whistling. Lo and behold,
within seconds, the dam burst and I gained blessed relief.

When the nurse arrived back with the catheter, she asked
Eoin what on earth he was doing. He stopped whistling to
explain, and immediately I stopped performing. The poor
girl must have thought we were a right pair of nuts because
she left us with her tray of equipment and a broad smile on
her face. And so Eoin returned to his whistling and I to the
painful job on hand.

Now, why on earth did Eoin's uncle want mares to urinate, the best part of fifty years ago? Surely there was no
such thing as pregnancy testing then? But Eoin has very
clear memories of learning that mode of whistling, under his
uncle's tutelage, as the older man stood with a galvanised
bucket at the ready.

At Eoin's next performance, and mine too of course, two
nurses came in to watch the show. Now, lying in bed, even
thinking of that whistle, makes me want to go. So I am not
at all surprised that those girls started to jiggle about a bit
too and quickly left us. But I was surprised when Eoin
offered his services, for any female on their corridor who
was in trouble with her waterworks and in need of assistance!

I intend to give Eoin a surprise when he gets in tomorrow,
our ruby anniversary. I have booked the hospital hairdresser

to come and do something with my hair — white roots and all. She also said that she'd give me a full make-up while she's at it. So he should have another reason to whistle, because, while he was whistling for me on the loo, unless he is blind altogether, I must have reminded him more of his uncle's old grey mare who won several medals at the Dublin Show in the 1930s and died of old age, than of the bay filly at home that bears my name, having been born on my birthday.

The Return of the Prodigal Son

My prospects for this Christmas were looking bleak enough all along. The highlight was to be my Christmas turkey and ham, a form of meals on wheels, from Sara. And, since all the families were busy asking Eoin what on earth to get me, I wasn't looking forward to anything much in the line of surprises either. Indeed, a bad case of self pity was just looming on the horizon, threatening to put a damper on everyone.

Then, our Christmas cheer came early, bringing us a great deal of happiness, when my son Seamus, and his youngest son, Justin, flew in from Los Angeles, last weekend. I couldn't believe it when I got the call to say that they were coming and would be here for a week, until early on Christmas Eve. It was quite unexpected. I knew Seamus wanted to come to see me when I was first in hospital but it wasn't practical.

He came, instead, when I really needed him. Apart from me being stuck here in this bed, there is also that indefinable sense of loss, deep down, about missing family members, which is always inclined to surface especially around Christmastime. Memories of Christmases past, seen through rose-coloured spectacles, crowd in to remind ageing parents

of what, in retrospect, was a truly happy period. The fighting, the disappointments, and the sheer hard work of it all
are completely forgotten.

It has been a great comfort to me, these past few days, to
lie here, listening quietly as three of my sons reminisced
together about their childhood. Usually, when so many of us
are together, there is some upheaval or other, and harsh
words are exchanged. Then they remember all the things
that we, as parents, did wrong. Or long-ago sibling thefts of
personal property are resurrected, with recriminations about
music tapes or favourite jumpers that once, mysteriously,
disappeared without trace.

This time, fortunately, the talk was more on the fun and
freedom they had, as children, in comparison to their own
children nowadays. And I, lying either on my bed or on a
couch in front of the fire, learned more about their escapades
than I ever knew before. Some of their stories stood the hair
on my head, like the time that all five of them took a sit
upon lawnmower, a mile and a half, to the nearest village,
just to buy a block of ice cream.

Seamus claimed to have been the instigator of that plot
— surprise, surprise — so he got to drive the lawnmower.
The two youngest were put in the grass box so that they'd
be safe, he said, and the other two were perched one on
either side of him hanging on for dear life to the back of the
seat. It must have been all most highly dangerous. Eoin Óg
then added that he now knows that one father in the parish
used to come into dinner regularly at his house and say, as a
warning to his own family, that the Kavanagh boys would
surely all be killed at the rate they were going.

Then, and only then, did I find out all the things they
used to get up to when bringing home the loads of straw we
used to buy all over the parish. They'd arm themselves with
great bags of apples for each trip — some to eat, but mostly
for ammunition. When high up on the load, they'd use the
apples for target practice, and no dog, passing cyclist or car

roof was safe. An elaborate scoring system made hitting a person worth ten roofs and so on.

So, it was no wonder the neighbours were talking about them, and just as well that Eoin is kind of deaf today. As story followed story, each one getting progressively worse, I, too, began to wonder how we ever reared them. But I also determined to remember those tales of their youth for when their own children are old enough to cause them real heart-break. Then, I might even have enough ammunition to explain one generation to another, if such a thing is ever possible.

Seamus, our then farmer-to-be, once broke our hearts when he was just barely seventeen and left home for good after a very troublesome period. That was our saddest Christmas ever. It is a wry coincidence that Alice Taylor, in her review of *Country Living*, quoted extensively of my pain at that turbulent time, just the week before that particular son came all the way from Los Angeles to make us so un-expectedly happy this Christmas. Little did I think, seven-teen years ago, that such a thing would ever be possible, or indeed that I'd ever be happy again. Nothing, however, is final except death. And I so very nearly was not here for this Christmas.

Cooking for Two

You'd hardly believe it but I am now eating better than I ever did before in my life. I lie here in the bed and, coming up to mealtimes, sniff the air to try and guess what is likely to come my way this time.

'I suppose the daughters-in-law are constantly running in to you with bowls of soup and titbits to tempt your appe-tite,' said a friend to me the other day.

'God help your head!' I replied, telling her instead what a marvellous cook Eoin has turned out to be, after four months' practice. But I don't think she fully believed me. Her own fellow, as she said, couldn't even boil a kettle.

Of course, he soon would, if he had to. But to develop an interest in cooking takes something more than sheer necessity. It also takes time. Indeed, the last time I was laid up for a long period, seventeen years ago, after my hysterectomy, Eoin kept me fed all right, with tea, bread and butter and frozen savoury pancakes. If I ever got fed up of anything in all my life, it was then, with commercially prepared frozen food. The only changes were rung with fish fingers, burgers and such like. I was dying for a good feed of potatoes in no time flat. So I was out of that bed quite quickly, to feed all. They were also suffering with Eoin making it into the kitchen from his work usually only a bare five minutes before the appointed meal time. And, in those days, workmen and the odd stray mechanic also got all their meals as a matter of course.

This time, however, Eoin brought home a book, *Cooking for Two*, which was really very suitable since there are now only the two of us to be fed. I smiled somewhat weakly, however, knowing only too well the fate of different cookery books I personally had purchased over the years. However, I was wrong. Eoin is working his way steadily through this book, ever since, page by page — that's why I never know what's coming at mealtime.

Thank God he never asks me what I'd like. I now know just why, whenever I asked Eoin that in the past, the only answer I ever got was, 'Whatever is the easiest, love.' I used to fume wondering why he either couldn't, or wouldn't, answer such a simple question. Now, with the boot on the other foot, Eoin's methodical approach to this whole business of cooking is quite an eye-opener for me.

Firstly, he has his shopping list of the exact ingredients needed for a few days ahead. The very first day he came in to me in vain, looking for all sorts of things I never had in my store cupboard. Anchovies and pink peppercorns were never stock ingredients in my style of cooking. Fortunately, however, I saw one list, which had, as an item, the zest of an orange. I could imagine his mortification if he went looking for that in the supermarket. I daresay, however, that some kind fellow shopper would have put him right there since he is constantly coming back to me with tales of the women who come to his rescue when he can't find something, or he chooses badly. He even had the temerity to ask me, after one shopping trip, if I knew how to test a melon for ripeness!

The same attention to detail is also carried into the kitchen because everything has to be laid out on the bench before he ever starts to cook. And he pours himself a glass of wine as well, in the best television tradition. Indeed, last Sunday when some old friends came to visit me, I was highly amused to find that Chloë and I were discussing pension plans at the bedside, while Eoin and Harold were at the base of the bed, swapping recipes and tips on cooking. I have always had that useful ability to listen to one conversation whilst taking part in another, which is fine until I find myself giving answers to the wrong conversation.

But this time I deliberately interrupted the two men in full flow because it suddenly struck me that so striking a role reversal should not go unregarded. I bet that forty plus years ago, when those two first became friends out hunting, little did they ever think they would be one day discussing sauces for different fish dishes. How much times, and they, have changed. Then, as young bloods, they followed the hounds, and both were the devil to go, I'm told. Now, they are retired from work and their former strenuous pursuits. Yet here they are with a great new interest in common.

Harold, we already knew, was a past master at the cookery game. He had even gone to a cookery course where he was the sole male present, not that that bothered him in the slightest. He threw a dinner party afterwards just to demonstrate his latest skills. The two other men present also admitted to a certain prowess in the kitchen. Eoin was the only one there who had to admit that while he had no hang-ups about cooking, he just found it impossible to synchronise all the different things to be ready together. Some items always finished up cooked to a mush while others were still half raw.

But now all is changed, changed utterly, and a terrible beauty is possibly about to be born. Eoin, Harold and another friend, David, have just signed up for a six-week cookery course in the local community school. The three musketeers won't be in it with them. I await the results with keen anticipation. Because, if all goes well, I may never return to full-time kitchen duties again. But all might also go horribly wrong, if any of the women on the course think that here are three womanless men and take too much pity on them. The supermarket encounters are brief. But a lot could happen in the space of six weeks!

Active in the Bed

The worst kind of bores are those who, when you ask them how they are, proceed to tell you at great length. We all know them. Indeed, one woman, whom we meet occasionally, is distinguished by Eoin as 'Mrs Stomach Murphy' because she always regales him, at length, with tales of all she has suffered with her stomach. It's cruel, I know, but there is no doubt but that some people do enjoy ill-health.

It sometimes amuses me, here in the bed, when I get a phone call, and, after perfunctory inquiries as to how I am doing, I then get full details of all the caller's ills. Not that that's a problem for me because, after all, there is nothing new about my slow but steady progress, and I do have an insatiable curiosity about other people's lives. And now, well into my sixth month flat on my back, vaginally dead, my personal life lacks excitement anyway.

But one thing I am doing, thanks to some of my good

friends, is redecorating my house from top to toe. Eoin says
I'm mad. But actually I think it is a very sane decision. Here
I am, sixty-one years old, and I never once got a professional
painter into the place. As a result, some interior teak doors
that were put in twenty-odd years ago never got even a lick
of varnish. Eoin and I ran out of steam somehow before that
job was finished. These are, therefore, still in their pristine
state — if you ignore all the greasy finger marks. It was
always just one of those many things we intended to get
around to some day.

But, above all, my bedroom was never designed as a
boudoir for receiving guests. So, for months, both before
people came to see me and after they left, looking around
me I kept deciding that really something drastic must be
done. 'Yes dear' or 'It's you they came to see not the bedroom' was the only comfort I got from Eoin. He just didn't
seem to see the stacks of books that must be breeding in
dark corners, the heaps of not-quite-finished-with newspapers, his personal stack of *The Field* ever growing, the
detritus of visiting granddaughters, and our recently discarded clothing draped on chairs too shabby for the rest of
the house.

I know I have a very handy gadget that picks up anything for me. Pádraig saw it one day recently in a chemist
shop while Sara was buying gripe water for Ciara, and he
decided it was just the thing for me. A knitting needle or the
TV remote control falling on the floor, out of reach, is now
no longer a minor disaster. So I could, in theory, tidy away
most of these things myself if put to it. But I wanted much
more than that. I wanted a complete change.

My next visitors happened to be two fellow members of
my Altrusa club. So I told them of the notion that was on
me. And, in no time flat, they were in there planning what
could be done here and what could be done there. They also
reminded me that one of the group is very talented at interior design — colour schemes and all that. So, next thing,

she was out as well, and I was up to my eyebrows, in the bed, with colour cards, wallpaper books and other essentials.

It was all heady stuff. Ideas flew. I always thought that interior designers were for the birds — who would want everything ripped out to start afresh? But not a bit of it. What I really needed, I was told, was a little re-organising. For example, I was told that my curtains would hang better if they had good tape and not the cheapest kind on the market. And hems should be sewn and not just pinned! I, of course, always made my own curtains — like my mother before me — but I didn't dare say that out loud. And I learned how to wallpaper and paint under my mother's eagle eye as well. Each sheet of paper had to match exactly, and woe betide us if any air bubbles weren't properly smoothed out with circular rubbing motions.

Poor old Eoin didn't know what hit him when he brought us in coffee and biscuits, which, through lack of a suitable table, we had to have on the end of the bed. I had, of course, already told him of the notions that were on me. But he hadn't really taken me seriously — just humoured me by telling me to go ahead and do whatever I wanted. He thought he was quite safe in that, that I'd talk and talk but never get around to doing anything about it.

A phone call, however, had already been made to a painter who could start the very next day, since he was between jobs. Otherwise it would be at least two months because he had a very big job in hand. So Eoin was asked what would he think of various colours, and highlighting the beams of our old hipped ceilings with darker tones of the same. From the bemused look on his face, I knew he hadn't a notion of what we were on about, all talking together as we were. But he did say that he could see no real reason why the painter couldn't start next day, downstairs.

So here I am, in my old bedroom, with the smell of paint wafting though the door every time it is opened. Things are moving at the rate of knots. My curtains are all gone to be made over by a genius with a sewing machine. Another friend says she can't wait to bring out just the kind of really big lamps that an old house like this needs. And if I don't like them, there is no harm done. Just as there was no harm done when another member, with connections in the antique trade, brought out tables that she said were just what I needed. They were too ornate, by half, for my taste, and pocket. But there was no bother about taking them away again.

So, all in all, I am frightfully busy at the moment. As soon as the spare room is finished, I'll move out there and let the transformation commence here. As for the family, all I have told them is that I am spending some of their inheritance. And why shouldn't I?

The Decorating Chicken Comes Home to Roost

I thought that by a wave of my hand from my bed and signing the cheques, I'd have no bother in getting my house looking like something out of *House Beautiful*. It has not been quite that simple, however, even though I have already signed more cheques than I'd really expected and I'm still not finished. It is the old, old story of one thing leading to another.

It was a mad notion to redecorate the whole house anyway. You might even say it was a sick notion on the part of a sick woman whose every whim was being humoured in order to keep her happy. I can tell you this much for nothing, however. If we were back to that first day, weeks ago, when my friends came and the whole redecorating notion was hatched, I'd say that Eoin wouldn't even open the door for them. He is sick to death of carting furniture around. Men never do understand, even at the best of times, that the

only way to know how things will look is to try them out in
different positions in the various rooms. And this applies to
pictures and ornaments, as well as furniture.

The whole house is disturbed, especially the poor spiders.
There sure were plenty of those about. And why wouldn't
there be when, apart from our bedroom, nothing else had
been touched since that day I fell in September? When the
first of the spring sunshine highlighted the curtains of cob-
webs over the bed, I got Eoin to tackle those, all right, with
an old shirt tied about a sweeping brush.

But God help the rest of the spiders in the house when
the professional painter got to work. They quickly disappeared, I'm told, into his vacuum cleaner, together with
much newly exposed dust and dirt. And all this was taken
away with him each evening, for disposal elsewhere, so
there was no getting in again for those spiders anyway.
Eoin's earlier spider clearance had consisted of a shake of
his brush out the window.

It's a wonder the girls didn't help you with that?' com-
mented someone to whom I had told the story of Eoin and
his spiders. But she was talking from the perspective of the
mother of daughters and not that of daughters-in-law. Her
daughters would have no problem about taking a sweeping
brush in their hands when visiting their mother and setting
to with a will, wherever they saw the need. But it is not that
easy for daughters-in-law, slow as they'd be to give offence.

True enough, some women would take it as a criticism
for another woman, regardless of the relationship, to take a
pro-active part in her cleaning problems. It is wrong to
presume that all people think alike. I learned my lesson on
that score when I got into severe trouble by being what I
thought was helpful to daughters-in-law, only to discover,
much later, that I had given great offence at the time. It took
me years to learn that mothers-in-law are always in the way.
The joke of the whole thing is that once I thought that we
could even share the same box of washing powder!

Now that I know better I wouldn't even dare water a flagging house-plant, not to mind offering advice as to how to prevent their imminent demise, although my fingers would itch to succour the needy.

Yet, if it came to pulling weeds in my garden, or indeed cleaning my house either, I'd be only too delighted were anybody to do anything at all for me in that line. Many years ago, when all my American family were staying here, one morning I was highly amused when that daughter-in-law asked my permission to clean our phone. We had no mobile phones in those days and it pained the poor girl greatly every time she had to use ours, which lived on the kitchen window so that all urgent farm calls could be made without coming into the house. There are no two ways about it. That phone was dirty. And I was more than delighted to see it being cleaned. But never, in a hundred years, would I have asked her, or any other daughter-in-law either, to do any cleaning for me. I am still working hard at keeping the zip on my lip tightly shut.

And I am quite sure that one day I am going to be the best mother-in-law in the world — once I am safely dead.

JANUARY

Welcoming in the New Year

How many of you lit the candle for the New Year? That custom seems to be vanishing faster than that of the candle on Christmas Eve. But I still follow the old tradition of a brand new candle for the New Year. Though I must admit that nowadays I only buy one-pound candles for both occasions.

Do you remember when buying only one-pound candles, at Christmas, by a farmer, was a sure sign of meanness, or else hard times, and both were worthy of comment? The local bright boys would also quickly decide which it was. So, it was essential that two-pound candles were specified on the list of messages if the woman of the house wasn't going shopping herself. They had to be two-pounders anyway to last, since they were lit every night between Christmas Eve and the New Year.

Here, the candle on Christmas Eve is always lit by the youngest in the house, accompanied by a suitable prayer for all the family, both living and dead. We kneel down, for the lighting, around the kitchen table. Long ago the woman of the house then took over for the New Year and the ceremony of the candle was much less. But this may have been because supper had to be seen to as well. Christmas Eve was always a fast day — stockfish and onion sauce with the potatoes at dinner time, and plain bread and butter with the six o'clock tea.

There was no fast, however, on New Year's Eve. Indeed it was vital to have a big feed on that night, to ensure no want for the year coming. As well, on the last night of the old year, just before supper, a freshly baked cake was thrown, with force, by the woman of the house, against the back door, to keep out hunger and want for the year ahead. This made sense, then as now, because hunger always comes through the back door. Hunger for farmers comes from not looking after one's business — the farm and the yard: those are always out the back.

The importance of the place of the farming woman, be she wife or widow, in keeping hunger at bay, was emphasised by the use of the right formula of words earlier employed at the lighting of the candle. They always went something like this, a demand not a request: 'We want famine to retire out of here, from this night right up until this night twelvemonths.' My mother dispensed with the cake-throwing ceremony but not with the prayer, or the candle lighting, as far as I can remember.

But I did see the cake both baked and thrown when I first married in here. And there would have been hell to pay those early years, before I got control of the kitchen, if I laid a hand to a sweeping brush after midday on New Year's Day. To do so would be to sweep out all our luck for the year. And, do you know, I have some city friends who, when they are sweeping their driveways, any day of the year, always sweep inwards and never just out onto the footpath. They may think they are being very civic minded, keeping their dirt at home, but I wonder. I'd safely say the roots of their habit go much further back.

We all had to be very careful as well, not to throw any scrap of food, even the smallest bit, outside the back door, all of New Year's Day. Even the dogs had to be fed inside. And the hens, always scratching about, could be fed only from foodstuff stored outside. The line was drawn at letting them into the kitchen. It was tempting fate, you see, to give anything away that day, much less throw anything out. Not even the tinkers would come to the door on New Year's Day for they knew it would be no good for them. They were not stupid. They knew they'd need us another day.

In those years we also had one character in the parish who was noted for being somewhat stupid or simple. I sometimes wonder, however, quite how simple he was; he had a great thing going for himself well into the New Year. He extended, of his own volition, the wren-boy custom, until he had the whole parish covered. And nobody once said to him that he was late with the wren. 'Sure God love him: he doesn't know any better,' was said instead as the purses were opened.

Johnny was even cute enough to retrace his steps selectively the odd time. And still nobody said no at this second call but put it all down to the lack in him, and opened their purses again. But Johnny would voluntarily stay at home himself on New Year's Day. He wouldn't step outside his own place because he wouldn't take our luck from us for the New Year.

With the benefit of hindsight, one can see that all the customs that marked out our hours also marked the time passing for us. Pure superstition it all was, of course, but these superstitions did give a structure to life. One could then 'know' things in a way totally alien to life today, when even the existence of God and Heaven is doubted.

Then we fully believed that the gates of Heaven were open to all for the twelve days of Christmas, just as we ourselves left our doors unlocked all that period for the Holy Family travelling the earth for a place to lay their heads. So those who died in this blessed time went straight to Heaven, regardless. The old people around used to say that only the good died at Christmastime anyway. Thus, in their own simple way, they resolved the theological quandary of there being this exception to the concept of hell and purgatory as inevitable and legitimate places of punishment for ill-doing here below.

However, nobody really wanted to test that tenet of faith

because everybody was secretly pleased with a hard, cold Christmas. 'A green Christmastime means a full church- yard,' was regularly said in the course of the everyday conversation about the weather. Nobody was too anxious to head for those open gates. And, if it did snow, we firmly believed that the angels were plucking their Christmas or New Year geese in heaven.

A new moon was the best of good luck at the New Year, once you didn't see it through glass. Of course you also turned over the money in your pocket at that moment, bless- ing yourself and saying a prayer for all the dear departed. Then you could be really sure of a very prosperous new year.

If the cock crowed at midnight on New Year's Eve, this was an even better sign of the year to come. The fact that the New Year was welcomed in, at midnight, by the ringing of church bells, and the parading of young men going from village to village, with every possible noise-making instru- ment they could lay their hands on, was sure to set all the cocks of the country crowing, of course. I well remember those early years of my marriage being woken up by the noise on the main road as the revellers went their way. But, alas, there is not a hen cock left anywhere now, and the young men no longer leave the pubs to frighten away the demons of the winter. They were the ones supposed to help spring to come in, with their noise and vigour.

But still, even without them, the daylight lengthens, by a cock's step every day, from New Year's Day onwards. We slowly change our customs but the eternal rhythms do not change. I sometimes wonder if I am one of the very last to retain any vestige of the old customs. My daughter-in-law's house is already bare of decorations. Yet not a sprig of holly will be shifted while I am mistress of this house until Nollaig na mBan, the Women's Christmas, is safely over. I will light my pound candle again the night before, and tell Michaella how water is supposed to be turned to wine at midnight, rushes to silk and gravel to gold.

Next day, all my holly and ivy will come down. I will keep the one piece of holly, however, next to the sprig of blessed palm from last Palm Sunday, even though I no longer have an open fire on which to cook the first pancake on Shrove Tuesday night. The palm will stay until it is replaced by the new spray, next Palm Sunday. Come what may, however, the old one cannot then be simply thrown away. It must be burned in the same way as surplus holy medals, and the like, must always be consumed by fire.

Sometimes they do amuse me — the holly and the palm, the sacred and profane — as they wither away there, stuck over the picture frame, side by side. Of course I am not superstitious. I suppose, however, I am just a little bit like that apocryphal old woman who, when asked by a folklorist did she believe in fairies, replied, 'Indeed I do not, sir. But they are there all the same, sir....'

Did He Ketch You Then?

'There's not much room in farming for sexual harassment anyway and that's for sure,' said one of my visitors this week as we discussed the state of the nation. 'Sexual harassment is all a load of nonsense anyway, as far as I can see,' he went on, because, of course, it was a he.

'I would safely bet that you never had a problem, Liz, at any stage during your lifetime ... or any other decent woman I know either,' he concluded, glancing at his wife as though he had now said all that there was to be said on the matter. So I had to take issue with him on the spot.

'Did none of the boys at national school have a go at "ketching" you then, Mary?' I sneakily asked his wife, knowing full well the answer since we were almost contemporaries there. And then, I found myself blushing just at my use of the word 'ketch' — it has such unpleasant, even shame-making memories for me. I presume it was just the local pronunciation of the word 'catch', but it was used in very specific circumstances as when a male made a grab at a female between her legs. To grope I suppose is the modern slang term for the same sort of sexual attention/ harassment. It is a moot point as to which term best explained it.

For me, however, it was downright harassment and began at our national school, as I grew older. There, the noxious dry toilets were out of view of the school windows, to the side of the official tiny playground. The real, but unofficial, playground was a steep field, past the toilets. This field the boys tried to maintain as theirs and theirs only, leaving us girls to play hunt or thread the needle in the front. Unfortunately, we had, occasionally, to go to the toilet, and some particularly big boys would always be lying in wait around the corner to 'ketch' any girl who ventured near.

But some of the bigger girls, inexplicably to me, used to run the gauntlet again and again, allowing themselves to be hastily grabbed at. They would then come running back to the playground, roaring laughing. They used to tease us younger ones unmercifully too, saying, 'Did he ketch you then?' if we went anywhere within the vicinity of any boy, and not just the gropers who by no means confined their activities to just around the corner. We never felt safe, and being teased, in mocking terms, if we were unfortunate enough to be caught, added downright shame to our actual physical discomfort.

This activity was not confined to the so-called children at national school. Remember that then only a tiny minority went on to any further schooling. Therefore, these boys and girls were well into puberty and they still had to stay on at national school. And anyway, they were only putting into action there what they saw outside. Public groping, with the girls giggling and laughing loudly in encouragement, running away only to come back again, was very commonplace in the city or country, wherever young people gathered.

I was a late developer and all this activity was a complete mystery to me. I knew only that I objected very strongly indeed to it. The biggest trouble I ever got into at national school was when I stood up for my personal integrity, and, in my last year there, fought back at a groper, physically. He had grabbed at me in the playground in front of the school, neutral territory, so I was really mad and flew at him like a wild cat, scratching and kicking.

He fought back, slapping me about and I was coming off by far the worst of the battle, with a bloodied nose, when the Master, obviously seeing the fight through the window, came to intervene and cut short the playtime for everybody. Hauled up in front of everybody in the classroom, though shamed, I had no words to explain just why the fight began. When questioned, I had to admit that I had struck the first blow. I wonder now, however, how much that teacher either saw or suspected, because even though my assailant got a terrible beating, I was spared the stick on that occasion.

But my parents were told of my unladylike behaviour. So, I was made feel ashamed, all over again, but this time it was because I — a farmer's daughter — actually demeaned myself by fighting a farm-labourer's son. My parents never asked me just why the fight had really begun. Little did my parents know either that I had already tried my fists on one of our own workmen when he had tried to 'ketch' me as one day I took a ride in the butt with him across the yard. Never again would I go anywhere near him. But that did not stop him coming after me if I wasn't vigilant at all times. I surely hated him, venomously. But never once did I complain about him to my parents. I just grew handier and handier with my fists, sticks, stones, whatever.

That was the year I left home for boarding school, and all this receded into the distance, as something done by labourers, whom, it seemed, I should avoid for every reason. That particular red-headed workman was gone by Christmas anyway. We had a fair turnover of workmen in those years before my father died. Only Paddy was a constant, year in and year out. That is until the week after my father died and Paddy gave in his notice on the spot because no way would he stay working for a woman. 'They'd all make too much of a "hare" of me if I did,' was the only explanation he would ever give.

I never had to use my fists on Paddy. But, as my adolescence progressed its especially rocky way following my father's death, I soon found that it wasn't only boys I had to deal with. Now the gropers were grown men, and farmers to boot. Once, when I was fifteen or maybe just sixteen and never been kissed — possibly because of my ready fists — a neighbour came to call. He was very helpful to my mother in her early widow-hood and often came in the evening to see if we were doing all right and to play a game of a hundred and ten with us.

Anyway, this night, on his way into the kitchen to my mother, he met me on my way back in from locking in the hens, at dusk. It was a balmy and beautifully still summer's evening. All that was suddenly changed, however, when this old man suddenly grabbed hold of me and tried to kiss me. Taken completely by surprise, my temper rose with the vile smell of porter and the rasp of his white stubble on my face. With all my strength, I lashed out as hard as ever I was able into that porter-filled belly. He, of course, was doubled up and I still remember his rueful voice saying, 'But I thought that's what you'd be wanting by now, a great big girl like you....'

The fact that he was well nigh old enough to be my grandfather didn't come into the equation at all. Like many another bachelor in the countryside, the older he became, the younger were the girls he fancied. And, as a bachelor, I suppose he felt entitled to try his luck. But he never did again with me and that's for sure. I don't hold any grudge against him like I do against some of the men — farm-ers/contractors — who came to help my mother, those first years. I soon got to know those who weren't at all averse to running their hands up my bare leg under my skirt. When I

had to take their meals out to them in the fields I soon
learned to drop the basket and leave, once I was sure they
had seen me. Usually I just hung around, out of sight, until I
heard the tractor start up once more and it was safe to re-
trieve the basket.

My mother, in all of this, thought that I was getting too stuck
up to talk to the neighbours, and said as much to me more
than once. Yet I never complained even though I often did
grumble about the chore of having to get them their meals.

Come to think of it, only once, in all my life, did I ever
comment about any form of sexual harassment. And that
was only just last year. I was a guest in somebody else's house
when a fellow guest put his hands on my breasts, squeezing
painfully while asking, seemingly playfully, how come I was
so fat up there and not a pick on me anywhere else.

A knee in the groin was my preferred option to deal with the
situation. But I just couldn't do it, nor even use my fists as in
times of yore. It would cause too much commotion and great
embarrassment to our mutual host and hostess. So, I just left the
group I was in and moved to join another. There, in that mixed
group, I told my tale of modern-day sexual harassment. If I was
looking for sympathy, however, I was on the wrong tack. One
of the women just said that that was Dan's little way and to
take no notice at all of him. One of the men, however, asked me,
leeringly, if I didn't just love every moment of it. All — both
men and women — laughed heartily at that. I was discon-
certed because I knew quite well that I had probably embarrassed them all horribly by even talking about such things.

So I moved on, once more, to yet another small group where
the discussion was on farming — much safer ground. There is
no doubt, however, that a certain percentage of farming men
are no different from the rest of society when it comes to sexual
harassment. It is just less overt these days. And young girls, I
hope, are now able to use their tongues to complain and not
their fists. But I still have my doubts about the majority of
people being really willing to listen. Most women still put up

with a lot before they do anything about it. We just don't have the easy words to explain how we feel

Out to Sunday Lunch

Going out to lunch on a Sunday is such a civilised thing to do. I decided that this Sunday, when Eoin and I were out to lunch. The food was good. The conversation flowed easily and all in all I had a thoroughly good time, whatever about Eoin.

When we came home, however, I was hard set to explain to the young folk here just what it was that made our Sunday afternoon so enjoyable. We had eaten well and very leisurely. Obviously great care had been taken by our hostess over the finer details of the food and the service. Yet she was quite relaxed about the whole affair. Therefore, it was easy for us to be relaxed as well. I was reminded forcibly of the time we were at another house for dinner, and our hostess on that occasion, as Eoin later said, 'had a red face up on her like a turkey cock in stubbles', she was that fussed about the whole thing. She also kept apologising, to an embarrassing degree, for things nobody would have noticed if she hadn't called attention to them in the first place.

I explained all this and Lisa then asked, 'As you were so delighted with your lunch out, why is it that you never seem to have people yourselves here for lunch?'

That drew me up short because it was a perfectly logical question in the circumstances. Yet, I could not give a perfectly logical answer to it. At our time of life it would make perfect sense for us to invite people for lunch, instead of an evening meal, since we no longer like to eat late at night anyway. And, we also really suffer next day if things go on, and people just won't go home before two or three o'clock in the morning.

There is a lot less work in preparing a lunch as well. The only disadvantage could be that lamplight is kinder to people and their surroundings than is harsh sunlight. But, then again, maybe that isn't a total disadvantage either. The spiders and the dust are really only disturbed in my part of the house when visitors threaten. Indeed, if any of the family sees me cleaning house they immediately ask who is coming this time.

Really, the only acceptable answer I could produce for my daughter-in-law was that we were never used to entertaining in the middle of the day, simply and solely because there were always cows to be milked on a Sunday afternoon, as, indeed, on any other afternoon of the week. Sunday afternoon visitors were nothing but a nuisance, on that account, and never something we would wittingly draw on ourselves. I daresay we still find it hard to change the habits of a lifetime.

In my heart of hearts, however, I know that the reason goes deeper than that, way back in history in fact. Peasant papists do not have people in for Sunday lunch even though they may, at times, be invited out for luncheon at the homes of their Protestant friends. The only place we go to Sunday lunch is to a public restaurant. And, even then, such occasions are few and far between. Our colonial history is also evident when it comes to the foods we cook. Where is our native Irish cuisine? To this day it is 'Big House' food we cook for our dinner parties. Maybe this is why dinner parties can be so much real hard work. Do any of us ever use traditional Irish food and recipes for such occasions when we seek to impress? Would we indeed know how?

I don't think I ever made the traditional form of Irish stew, which uses mutton, potatoes and onion only, with no thickening agent or colouring. It sounds revoltingly greasy to me. Soda bread is about the only authentically Irish speciality I prepare. But that question of ethnic food and our colonial heritage, is getting into something much deeper than I set out to discuss here. I started off to tell you, as we did the family, an echo from the past which came back to haunt Eoin at lunch.

One of our old friends there started reminiscing about old times and the parties we all used to go to. He drew up again one specific party, in the 1960s, a fancy-dress party where we all had to go as members of the opposite sex: the men were all to choose female characters and the women male. The men were much better at that than we were. I, for instance, went as a Red Indian Chief, feather head-dress and all on my long black hair. Everybody but everybody, male and female, wore their hair long in the 1960s.

Eoin went as Twiggy, the very first of the long-legged, half-starved-looking fashion models. She was all the rage then. Eoin wore a wrap-around tartan mini-skirt of mine, which barely kept him decent. He wore his own white shirt tied in a knot about his waist, exposing just a hint of a hairy belly button. The whole ensemble was completed by the biggest pair of black tights we could buy, to cover that great expanse of hairy leg. He drew the line when I suggested shaving them, knowing as I did how the hairs would work their way through. Coloured ribbons were the best feminine slant I could manage for his size ten-and-a-half, shiny, black patent-leather evening shoes. These had been in the bottom of his wardrobe ever since the dress dances of the 1950s. I had also bought him a set of really fabulous, false fur eye-lashes, specially for the occasion. He really looked the part once I had him all made up.

Being Twiggy, he didn't need anything shoved down his chest. That was part of the joke, and possibly Eoin's reason to choose Twiggy in the first place. Other men there went as Mae West, Dolly Parton, Old Mother Riley and the like. They used pieces of rolled up clothing, cut out pieces of foam, footballs, or big balloons, depending on their choice of character. I know precisely what they used to make their curves because, as the night went on, there was the constant hilarious pulling out of things for display.

At some stage, however, when the night was well on and the bottles well lowered, Twiggy, talking to a rugby player, reached over and putting his hand firmly on the rugby jersey, asked in all seriousness, 'How on earth did you get yours as good as that? They feel so really real.'

He quite forgot, in all the cross dressing, and possibly a few drinks too many as well, that it was a woman he was talking to, albeit now a boyish rugby player in shorts. Fair dues to her, she took it well. Eoin was the one who died the death. All the way home he kept saying over and over, 'If it was only any one else but the vicar's daughter....'

Despite Eoin's kick in my shins under the table, I recounted that tale once more at our lunch party. All laughed uproariously, of course, but none more so than the man on my right. I thought he would explode. Finally, when he regained his composure, he asked please to be told more. But I'm positive his wife then aimed a kick at his shins, also under cover of the table. She was blushing as well. Her blushes were nothing to mine, however, when, despite her warning looks, her husband announced that he had married that vicar's daughter, pointing her out.

I can tell you that Eoin had a fair few cross words to say to me as we made our way home. But I would have to say that the vicar's daughter and her husband took my dreadful faux pas very well indeed.

Always Lie Through Your Teeth

During the week, someone I met out shopping, asked me how I liked my daughters-in-law — a leading question, if ever I heard one. So I gave my stock answer, which also happens to the true one, 'Better and better as the time goes on.' And I waited to hear her story, having thus carefully left the doorway of communication nicely ajar.

My friend is the mother of sons, with no daughters, just like myself. If I have one deep regret in life, it is that I do not have daughters. But she, being considerably younger than I am, is still at the stage of being inordinately proud of her four fine sons. She does not yet realise what she is missing. However, ever since her eldest son started going really steady with a girl, there are storm clouds on her horizon. And they broke in earnest after Christmas when that particular son asked his mother what she really thought of his girlfriend, who had come to stay for a few days.

'You didn't tell him I hope?' I interjected, a little too quickly. But, fortunately, she was still suffering too much, nearly a month later, to be put off that easily by a word in the wrong place.

'Well, I did,' she replied somewhat tartly. 'I never liked her anyway. From the very first time he ever brought her home, there was just something about her.... Now, I always swore I wouldn't say anything to him. But he did ask me for my honest opinion that night....'

My heart ached for her, because I didn't need her to tell me the rest of her story. I think each one of my lot has asked me that exact same question, more than once, about their various loves. And, it was only through bitter experience, I learned that the very last thing a son wants is an honest opinion from anybody — least of all from his mother — about the girl he loves at any particular moment.

Now, it was by far too late to advise my friend at this stage. The damage is done with her son. His loyalties have visibly shifted. She is deeply hurt because the last thing she expected was that he would go, and repeat to his girlfriend, word for word, what she had said. That to her was a form of betrayal on the part of her eldest son.

The girl, in her hurt, promptly packed her bags and left, taking the son with her. To say that communications have been strained ever since is putting it mildly. Of course, in time, they will all get over it. But a change has happened, whether he ever marries that girl or not. My friend, like every other mother of sons, or daughters either for that matter, will just have to learn to lie through her teeth, if needs be, when asked in future what she really thinks. Our children just do not want to know that. All they want is for us to confirm how marvellous, wonderful, enchanting and endearing their love object is.

All this we should know from years earlier anyway. Mothers have their major input only up to the age of ten or so. Then, if we are doing a good job, our children start growing away as they learn to become truly independent. The warning signs are clearly there for us all to see, from their teenage days on. And it is the wise parent who gets suddenly wary when sons and/or daughters begin to ask their parents' views about their friends, or even pop stars. The more critical you are of their friends, of either sex, or their current choice of idol, the more attractive you make them appear. All young people must buck their parents' opinions at that rebellious stage.

And nothing changes when they come to choosing a mate. It is fatal to go in for the direct attack, as my friend did. A sneaky approach is way better. Try to think of the nice things to say. Then, of course, if you are clever, you can slip in just the one thing that really concerns you most, keeping the very best point about the girl to follow on, immediately, to cushion that below-the-belt punch.

But that punch must be something that really concerns you, that you can articulate clearly, and it must also be a thing that something can be done about. Saying things like you don't like the girl because her eyes are too close together is pure nonsense and you are on a loser before you ever start. But my poor friend just doesn't like the girl. She wasn't able to pin down any particular point beyond that instinctive dislike. So she had harped on about the way the girl dressed, spoke, held her knife like a pen — didn't really fit in, in other words, to the mother's hopes and expectations for her son.

It was only by dint of questioning I discovered that what really upset her was the way that girl had taken free run of her house, without as much as a by your leave. She told me how it drove her mad to see the young lassie nonchalantly open the fridge and take out whatever she fancied without ever considering her hostess's plans for the next meal. She quite happily cut the first slice from a freshly baked cake on the table, before it ever got iced for the tea and visitors. And, eventually, a real complaint emerged — that the girl had gone into my friend's bedroom, sprayed herself with her perfume, and poked into drawers.

There, I thought, was the nub of the whole matter — the different expectations as to what was acceptable behaviour in a house guest. My friend has no daughters to make free with her possessions. So, to have had a stranger — and a rival for her son's affections at that — invading her privacy, as well as her domain, was her real cause of complaint.

As is my wont, I came out with the most direct question of all. 'How did you manage the sleeping arrangements?' I asked, since I know only too well that the sleeping arrangement when children bring home sexual partners for the first time, is the most common bone of contention of all. Most parents, even the most liberal, feel uncomfortable about their children sleeping with a partner under their roof although they may know, and even accept, that this is going on elsewhere.

'Now that's another thing,' came the quick answer. 'I gave her own room. But she didn't stay there. The lassie was brazen enough to spend the very first night in my son's room.' Oh dear! Oh dear! Oh dear! Why weren't the ground rules laid down first. Then, with the zip also on the lip, there might have been some hope, in the trickiest of all situations — the first meeting between mother and potential daughter-in-law.

FEBRUARY

'I've a Crow to Pluck...'

There were a few heated words at our country market this week, a somewhat rare occurrence, believe it or not. But when I was trying to calm down one of the protagonists privately — thus breaking one of my own rules — didn't she turn on me and bite the nose off me personally. She left me in no doubt at all of my failings and shortcomings, both as chairman of the market and as a person. Then, to add insult to injury she quite crossly remarked "Tis fine for you Liz ... nothing ever seems to bother you...!' as if that was what was really annoying her, the fact that I appear to let everything run off me like water off a duck's back. She felt that her suffering, because she had had a few cross words said to her by yet another member, was something quite unique to her ultra-sensitive soul. God help her foolish head.

With so many women running our country market there is bound to be friction from time to time as well as personality clashes. There are those who want prices up and those who think it better to sell in quantity at lower prices. Others then feel they have a right to keep their produce at the very front of the stall, and are willing to fight for their space, inch by inch. Of course, objections are occasionally raised.

I know that, personally, whenever I hear that high querulous tone coming into any woman's voice, I back off, if at all possible. Because, to join battle, and even prove to your own complete satisfaction, at least, how wrong the other is, doesn't help that peculiar sick sort of feeling at the base of your stomach.

There isn't a woman born, nor man either for that matter, who does not suffer a sick shock if unexpectedly attacked, be it by friend, foe or even stranger. Anybody bearding me with the expression, 'I've a crow to pluck with you...' always causes my tummy to turn over, no matter how completely innocent I feel with regard to that particular individual.

I suppose we are all conditioned, as social animals, not to have any friction with non-family members. Otherwise, why does any such conflict have an effect on us way beyond the cause? Just think of what can be said to you by your children, siblings or spouse and yet you never get quite that same feeling of shock when they attack. Perhaps this is because you grow quite used to their verbal affronts, if my teenaged children are the normal run of the mill. And I do remember absolutely detesting my own siblings at times, and telling them so too, to their faces. Yet, in my lifetime anyway, such rows in a family situation are quickly over and done with. They do not seem to break the taboo deeply ingrained in us against public scenes. Although that taboo does seem to be more deeply ingrained in some than others!

Time is the only cure when you know by the tone of voice that somebody is all out for a fight. A sweet smile doesn't help, because we all know quite well how infuriating that can be to somebody rearing for battle. Ever since I took over the chairmanship of our local country market I've had a great training in tactics. Indeed, I must say, now that my year in command is drawing to a close, that I have become very adroit indeed at side-stepping trouble.

I sure learned the necessity to delegate everything, even ideas. No matter what idea for the improvement of the market I came up with, someone always said, 'Sure I always said that.' Or else it is 'I know somebody else suggested that before, ages ago, at a meeting, and it was turned down flat then too....' Immediately then I knew that I was fighting an up-hill battle to get my idea accepted. However, if I presented a plan, whatever it was, as somebody else's great idea, of which I approved, as did many others, immediate support was guaranteed. There seems to be an unwitting desire in us all to diminish the top-dog, and also to be part of the winning group. One instinct cancels out the other easily, if the top-dog, or indeed even the top lady-dog, keeps a very low profile.

Lesson number two followed on from the first. This is always to keep out of the firing line at all costs, by this time delegating complaints instead of ideas. Never ever should the chairman do the correcting herself — she should always get somebody else to do it. At the same time, however, it is fatal to chastise like with like. I quickly discovered in my first few days just how disastrous that can be.

A man telling another man that his garden produce isn't up to scratch, over-priced or whatever, causes the hackles to rise on both men very quickly. The same message, from a gently spoken female, especially if she be reasonably young and attractive, works a treat, however. It is chancing it a bit to send an older woman, because that can have overtones of bossy mothers or teachers, and the hackles are out again.

I have also been known to play the nationality or religious card as well. We all do lean over backwards not to upset those different from ourselves, even when there is a bit of the 'Sure God help us — they don't know any better!' in our concern. I have always noticed at the market that Protestants are much nastier to each other, just as Catholics are to Catholics, than Protestant to Catholic or Catholic to Protestant. So too are Irish to Irish and English to English and so on. But it did interest me to note that Irish Protestants as well as Irish Catholics do not take very kindly at all, to any English correction, especially if the accent is of the 'wrong' sort. Could all this be remnants of old tribal enmities or post-colonial complexes?

Social background is also vital in my manipulations

(social class, of course, being a forbidden expression these days). If the person administering the corrective word is from the same social background, or somewhat lower, the 'Who does she think she is?' syndrome surfaces very quickly. I find the whole thing absolutely fascinating, both to observe and manipulate. It is a pity in a way that so few crows do emerge to be plucked at the market on Fridays! I hope to try a few more moves before my year is over — German/ French interactions for instance.

This week's problem, however, must first be resolved. One woman complained bitterly to me of the behaviour of another member's children in the coffee area. She demands that I, as chairman, sort it out before the next market, or else...! Now I wonder just to whom I shall delegate that particular problem. It's a far trickier one than any other little market dilemma so far in my year. I definitely do not want to be around if that crow gets to be plucked

Bigotry Imbibed at Birth

We had a visitor at the weekend, from far-off New Zealand, via the 'wee North'. He has gone, but I still feel vaguely disturbed after the visit and it is not from having a stranger to stay. God knows, I'm getting used to that by now.

I don't know if any body else suffers from sons who scatter invitations, as my lot do, literally to the far corners of the globe. I suppose it is a great temptation, when enjoying hospitality at some far away spot, to respond by saying that you must come and stay in my home whenever you get to Ireland. Haven't I done it myself, when only in far distant corners of Ireland? Both sides, however, usually know full well that this is just a form of politeness and that the people concerned will never call.

However, abroad, these casual invitations appear to get

passed on to friends and even friends of friends, as proved to be the case with this particular young man. On the phone he asked to speak to Pádraig who, of course, was in New Zealand all last year. On being told that he was away at the Mart, he said he was in the area and asked could he call.

'Certainly,' was my immediate response, because the kindness shown to our son, by total strangers, in New Zealand, is something we will never repay adequately. Odd, isn't it, that, even though our children are now all adults, it is we, the parents who feel responsible? It is as if the social debt was ours and not our children's — which is just as well here, because frequently our sons' reactions are anything but hospitable. Too often anyway, those guests turn out to be totally unknown to them personally; they may be years older than them; and they finish up as being our guests and our responsibility. It is a good job that this old house has such thick walls, so that the uninvited guests can't hear my whispered demands that my sons take them out from under my feet, especially when it comes to the night-time.

So I was not really surprised by Pádraig's reaction when he came home from the Mart. 'Never heard of him!' he brusquely dismissed me. 'But he'd better not be staying, for I've a dinner dance tonight.'

My heart sank at this, and it sank even further when the New Zealander arrived. He was obviously expecting to stay, bag and baggage, and, worst of all, he was obviously a good ten years older than my lads.

'Did your family know Pádraig in New Zealand? Was he farming with them?' I asked, hoping for common ground. It was so much wasted effort, however. Our New Zealander knew nothing about farming. Indeed, it next transpired that our address had come to him only via a girlfriend, Fiona Smith, of his own younger sister.

'Tell us more,' I said, because I had never heard the name Fiona mentioned before so I was naturally curious. I am under no illusions that I am told everything anyway. I am just grateful for the snippets I do hear and I try not to pry. I've always found that the less questions I ask, the more I am told. The trick, with sons anyway, is to display just enough interest to keep the conversation going, but to avoid at all costs any sort of a direct question.

However, with visiting strangers, one can question away. It keeps the conversation flowing for one thing. It transpired that this young man, Martin, was born in New Zealand of North of Ireland parents, and he had taken a year off work to do the round-the-world thing and to look up his grandmother and other relatives in the Six Counties. So, naturally enough, during the long night while we poured whiskey into him and wished for bedtime to come, we started to discuss the situation there, in Belfast, where he had spent the previous two months with his relatives. I asked him how he felt now about the sectarian divide, coming as he did from the other side of the world.

'I feel no different really, Mrs Kavanagh,' he replied, his accent suddenly becoming more Northern, 'because, thank God, in all those eight weeks there I've only spoken to two Protestants!'

Honestly, we were dumbfounded, this being the last thing we had expected to hear. Out of the corner of my eye I saw the cork being decisively put back in the whiskey bottle, by Eoin, when, in reply to my query as to how that could possibly be, he quite seriously went on to explain how totally separate the two sides were and what a good job that was. No relation of his, he said, would ever as much as pass the time of day with anybody in an RUC uniform, or frequent a Protestant bar or shop either.

Oh dear! oh dear! oh dear! What a lot those parents back there in Auckland have to answer for. The more this young man talked, the more bitter and black a bigot he showed himself to be. No way could the past eight weeks living in the North have so coloured this young man's way of thinking. Such bitter black bigotry must have been imbibed with his mother's milk — conditions in the North, as bad as they were, could not have done this damage in so short a time. He had never been there before. His parents had left there all right when religious discrimination was at its height, in the early 1950s, and doubtless they suffered their own share before they left. But they brought every bit of their hatred with them, and now, here, we had it epitomised in our own sitting room all those years later. That black hatred had grown, not diminished, over time and space.

Things did not improve for the rest of the weekend. Never, in all my years, have I inquired the religion of any person who came into my house. It just doesn't arise. I know some of my sons' friends are Protestant only because I know their parents. But others I really do not have a notion what religion they are, especially those with names that could easily be either. Martin was the first person ever to ask me the religion of many of the young people who were in and out of the house over the weekend. Yet when I told him straight out, while still keeping my hospitable face on, that I'd never asked he told me bitterly that it was all right for us Catholics here, we were never the downtrodden minority.

Then, being really naughty, without telling him their background, I took him to visit some Church of Ireland friends who have a New Zealand connection.

But I may as well have been idle. Martin is back off to his 'wee North' in the morning, as sure as ever he is right to hate. The reason he can't stay any longer with us, he explained, is that he collects his unemployment money the day after. He signed on once he arrived in Belfast, he told us, thanks to his uncle who put him straight.

I said no more. I kept all my opinions to myself, polite hostess and all that I am. But I sure do wish that my sons would keep their invitations to themselves until the time that they have both houses and wives of their own. As for Eoin, he took the cork out of the whiskey bottle again, in celebration, once Martin was safely gone.

My Personal Demon

It must be the masochist in me that insisted, last spring, in taking yet another piece from the nearby field to make my garden even bigger. Now this week I wish to God I never had a garden at all because there is so much to do in it and I am unable to anything. It upsets me even to think of doing anything. There is nothing physically wrong with me so I should be mad anxious to be up and doing on every front.

I find it difficult even to drag myself out of the bed these days. In bed one is not expected to think. Thinking brings fear. My gut instinct is to stay in the bed, curtains closed, duvet well up and the remote control in hand. The television, up good and loud, helps prevent thinking, as does reading the most trashy novels I can lay my hands on.

Now I know quite well what is wrong with me, but that knowledge does not make my present situation any easier. That old demon depression is nibbling at my edges once more. And I always know it is coming when I start to lose all pleasure in my garden as well as everything else. I haven't even seen Michaella for at least ten days and I feel no tug to go for her. So my symptoms are classical. A recent study showed that 92 per cent of depressed people no longer derive gratification from some major interest in their lives and 64 per cent experience a loss of feeling for other people.

Knowing my personal demon is coming makes it only marginally easier to manage. I have been to my doctor and have started on my anti-depressant tablets once more. But they have not kicked into action as yet. That is another cause for anxiety — the fear that this time they may not work. How to cope with the coming day is the uppermost thought in my head each morning on awakening. I only wish I could retain the merciful oblivion of sleep, permanently. I am more than 'half in love with easeful death' and that's for sure.

It is that awful anxiety, that unreasoning anxiety, that is

so hard to explain to anybody who does not suffer from depression. It is like a physical presence there with you, every minute of the day, sucking every bit of pleasure out of the most ordinary things in life. Even eating becomes difficult with that lump in the throat that comes each time one tries to swallow. I know it sounds stupid but I have often stood in front of the mirror, to try and see how big is that lump. But of course there is no lump.

When my bout of depression is over, it is easy enough to remember the things like that, the fear and awful anxiety. But the vulnerability caused by that demon depression, nibbling constantly at one's edges, becomes something past and obscure once it is over. This feeling of vulnerability is as hard to recall in sharp detail as it is difficult, in retrospect, to remember physical pain. Depression is such an agonisingly lonely journey that even those who have taken it cannot later compare their treks through the valley of despair.

Therefore it is not surprising that friends and family find it difficult to be sympathetic when needed. And, above all, they find it hard to accept that one must just stay on medication for a lengthy period. Instead they tell you to snap out of it, get busy, get a life. That lack of sympathy is particularly hard for older people to bear when the worries of the world are no longer supposed to be on their shoulders. And depression does strike particularly hard at the old. Eoin, as usual, is marvellous. He never says 'Pull yourself together, woman, and just get on with your life', which was what one doctor said to me once in the past — the dim and distant past. He, of course, is no longer my doctor.

The main trouble with accepting that one suffers from depression is that those who have never suffered from it are certain in their own minds that it results from some trauma or other, and, in their kindness, are hell bent on finding out what it is, so as to remove it, if possible. Money worries, family relationships going wrong and overwork are the conclusions most people jump to. Only yesterday I was strongly advised to give up this college nonsense — that the stress of studying for a degree, at my age, was what was wrong with me.

But, on the contrary, I think the reason I am able to fight back, to a degree, is that I have my garden, my writing, and in latter years, the necessity of keeping up in college even through it was also said to me that I was only there for a 'besting match'. I also now have a doctor who understands when I need help and I both look for it and take it.

A Kindred Spirit

Last Friday we had a cow off her feed in the parlour — always a bad sign. She was calved two weeks — nothing untoward in the calving, no mastitis as far as we could judge, no trace or smell from the vulva of a retained cleaning either, but she was definitely wrong. The ears were flat, the eyes were sunken, temperature subnormal. I personally am always happier if the temperature is up in any animal because I know then they are fighting the infection, whatever it is. But when it goes subnormal the prognosis is usually not good. Anyway I could see death in her eye. The family laugh at me here when I say that. But just by looking at an animal you can tell a lot. And they do get that hopeless resigned look in the eye when they have stopped fighting for life, and that I hate to see.

They also have another kind of settled look about them when they are safely in calf, long before there are any signs of the pregnancy showing. Equally, there is a sleek, polished look to a cow that is not in calf, regardless of the fact that she has not been noticed bulling, and so, for lack of any evidence to the contrary is presumed to be in calf. Those ones not in calf have a racy go to them, head up, game for any devilment; those carrying a calf move in a much slower and more placid way. Most unscientific way to go about things, I know, no wonder my sons laugh and say we should really be having them scanned, but that costs money. Yet I find it difficult to point out to my men-folk exactly what I mean by a placid, pregnant look. But I do recognise it. Then as the calving year goes on and a question arises about the cows to cull out for infertility, if I do not want them to sell some particular cow I bet the gang here that she is in calf. They frequently go along with me and don't sell her, that time anyway, just for the satisfaction of proving me wrong. And I have never had to pay up yet. But then again I have never collected on any of my bets either.

But there is such a thing as a natural stockman's eye — and women I contend, develop it to a higher degree than men. It is too soon to be sure, but I think Lisa could be de-veloping it. She definitely has a feeling for animals anyway. She tells Eoin Óg, these nights, that such a cow or such another cow looks likely to calve.

'I asked her, the first few times, was she mad or what, that the pins were still up and no trace of milk. But, to please her anyway, I put them in and blow me don't they always seem to calve before morning. I just don't know how she does it. But she told me she sees it in their faces,' Eoin Óg explained proudly.

But to get back to that sick cow in the herd. The sons de-cided she should be shifted out of here fast before she lay down and died on us. But it was Friday and not a meat fac-tory near us was killing. So, there was nothing for it but to bring her down to a separate pen, call the vet, and try to keep her alive till Monday or Tuesday and see could we shift her then. The men said it was a waste of good money on vets and drugs, but Lisa had an ally in me. She said that we just had to do something. Anyway, the vet came and eventually discov-ered that the problem was a retained cleaning, so far in that nothing at all showed externally. But he gave us practically no hope — she was completely toxic. Anyway, he pumped her full of antibiotics, and said that her only chance was to get her to drink a lot of Lectate in warm water. He did say to cut off the water drinker to make her drink from the bucket instead, but sure the cow was stretched out long before he came and personally I doubted she would ever rise again..

So Lisa took on the care of the cow. Shortly afterwards, I was out and, glancing over the wall, I saw Lisa sitting on the ground, with her arm around the cow's neck, talking to her and willing her to drink the Lectate concoction. And, with great delight, I was told she had drunk half of it. Well, before the weekend was over, she had drunk the full box of the sachets, and regularly I'd see Lisa — morning, noon, and in the middle of the night too at times, if we turned on the cameras — sitting, again with her arm around the animal's neck, and placing little titbits of silage, meal, grass fresh pulled from a paddock, and even tender young ivy shoots into the cow's mouth. And all the time, large conversations were going on.

I had told her about the ivy because I have often noticed that a sick animal that has refused everything else will nibble at ivy — for whatever reason, I don't know. And my only other input was to tell them to give her a calf as well, even if they had to feed it milk down there. The maternal instinct is marvellous. It gives a sick animal the will to live if it has a calf to look after. And didn't Lisa know the very calf that cow had had herself, which was more than I would have done, and brought it down to her. The cow appeared to recognise it and made no objections to us lifting her leg to let the calf get at her dug. Then, on Sunday morning, when we got home from Mass, Lisa rushed in to tell us that the cow had stood. And you know, I knew exactly how she was feeling. The satisfaction is marvellous when one is young and makes something live against the odds. As you grow older and wiser, you work out the economics of it all — the value of an animal after a really bad illness is not much. If sold it would probably be condemned at the factory. With this cow her milk will probably be gone, and she may lie down and die on us, at any moment, in the weeks if not months ahead. So common sense says shift them always. But still I am glad.

MARCH

Not Being a Superwoman

Is there anything more depressing to the spirit than excellence? Of course, it is somebody else's excellence I find so distressing. For me, personally, I doubt if excellence will ever prove more than a mirage, an impossible dream. Everyday, instead, I just seem to survive from crisis to crisis.

These are not earth-shattering crises, I know, to any outsider looking in. But still, like today, when the crowd of them were at the table, forks in hand, and the potatoes were still rock-hard in the middle — that was shattering enough to my self-esteem. No matter how often I speared different ones, my fork still told me that they were not yet done. What was I to do in those circumstance? I could strain the pot-full, anyway. But I knew only too well that that would result in cries of 'They're all hard — again!' with, of course, great emphasis on the 'again'. My only real choice is to let the potatoes, and my hungry crowd, simmer away.

This all happened because I wasn't in to put the potatoes down in time. Still, there have been other occasions when I put them down, extra early, to ensure that, for once, there would be no cause for complaint. But a phone call at the wrong time, or I just go out to do one little job in the garden, and next thing I find that I am straining a pot of mush. So, once again, I have a crisis on my hands with a hungry crowd in the door and not enough whole potatoes to go around.

See what I mean about going from crisis to crisis.

Now, later today I had to call into a neighbour's house with a message and I was pressed to come in. I did, out of pure curiosity, never having set foot in that house before. In her spotless kitchen I was offered tea with no less than two kinds of cakes, apple tart,-and she made sandwiches as we chatted, and the crusts were cut off as well. She herself had not a hair out of place. And her children, girls admittedly, were so polite, and above all so quiet.

Quite honestly, all that excellence depressed me thoroughly. I came home, well fed, but cross and upset with myself, wondering why I can never succeed in being a superwoman. Still — I then consoled myself — luck must have something to do with it as well. Nobody ever drops in on me when I have just indulged in a baking binge. They all seem to wait until all the tins are empty. Then I try to get some scones, unobtrusively, from the freezer and into the oven. I don't always find what I know is somewhere in my freezer, and even when I do, sometimes I know I have booped again when the frozen expression on my guests' faces matches the frozen centres of my seeming fresh, hot-from-the-oven scones.

Usually too, it is the very day that I am tempted to leave the dinner pots to soak and the floor unswept, that somebody chooses to call at the backdoor. I hate it when I have no choice but to take them into the disarray. Why, when everything is all clean and shiny, with fresh, spring flowers just picked and cakes just baked, does nobody ever choose to call? It is just another of the unsolved mysteries of my life.

There is no mystery in determining my real problem, however. That is that I am constantly chasing my own tail — doing one job while thinking of the next. The fact that I am up to my eyebrows in calves at the moment does not help one little bit. I always get the job of calf-feeding simply because, with all due modesty, I make a much better job of the calves than the men do. It must be the old maternal instinct coming out in me.

It has always been well known that women are undoubt-edly the best at looking after baby calves. A scientific study done recently merely confirmed this fact. In this study farmers' wives had by far the best results as regards mortal-ity figures and the general thrive of their charges. Farmers' daughters came second in the league table. Next came the farmers themselves, with hired help last.

I know who'd fare even worse than the hired help on that list and, oddly enough, they evidently were not considered at all. They should have been, because farmers' sons, if my lot here are anything to go by, have absolutely no patience at all with baby calves. Many's the time I've seen a calf's head forcibly dunked into a bucket of milk while the poor little thing was savagely told to drink it or drown! I've even seen a poor calf get a quick clout of a fist if its sharp little teeth gave the trainer's hand a bit of a nip. Sons' short supply of patience gives way all too quickly.

It is only too well I know how hard a job it is to get a calf to drink out of a bucket when its natural instinct is only to suck the pap of its dam. I do have some sympathy with the sons on that score. I can think of no more back-breaking work than bending over several baby calves in turn, trying to make them drink with the aid of your finger in their unwilling mouths. It is very hard to make calves understand that sucking a finger in all that wet stuff will be as good for them as sucking their mothers.

It is so downright frustrating, just as I have got a calf sucking, it gives a sudden puck to the bucket, just as it would to its mother, and milk cascades all over me and the calf, with some of it even trickling uncomfortably into my wellingtons. The only thing worse can be when I am bending over trying to get one going and another comes up from behind me to give me a savage puck in a very tender place indeed. The sons tell me that it is even worse for them, however, when this happens.

All males will desert the feeding of the calves on the

flimsiest of excuses anyway. So I bet I am not alone in the pain of being a calf-rearing farming wife in the spring. Still, when all this drudgery is over and all my calves are trained to drink well, it will be no time at all until I see my fine, sleek charges, galloping with mad joy, on their first day out to grass. Then I will know, with absolute certainty, that in one field at least, I have achieved excellence.

A Dream Come True

An extraordinary thing happened here this week. One of my long-held wishes came true without my doing a thing about it myself. In the early morning our farmer son came rushing in to say there was a peacock on the lawn. It sounded much too good to be true because peacocks are something I have long wanted in this place. Delusions of grandeur on my part, no doubt, but I have admired them so much when visiting the various stately homes on garden tours.

Eoin has often laughed at the good of it when I'd say, once again, that we really should do something about finding a source for peafowl. He knew only too well that I never even tried to make my dream come true, not even when he pointed out pea-chicks advertised in the small ads on the *Journal*, or our local paper. Eoin is a great one for reading every inch of all his papers. So, even though he might have no notion of either buying or selling a particular item, he still runs his eye down that column. He calls it getting his money's worth.

So really it wasn't lack of supply that prevented me from getting my peafowl. Maybe it was because I didn't know whether or not they were hard to keep — we do have foxes all over the place. Then again, anybody to whom I had mentioned that I'd just love a peacock or two around my humble abode told me that they'd do fierce damage to my garden, and that they were also extremely noisy birds.

Therefore, for one reason and another, or really no reason at all, peacocks remained one of my unfulfilled ambitions. Both Eoin and myself are past masters at putting things on the long finger anyway. Wishing alone, with no action taken, I know only too well, is not enough in this life. Still, for one minute, my heart fluttered in anticipation when Pádraig told us about the bird on the lawn — a peacock, he said it was. So, out we rushed, but there was no peacock to be seen.

We gave Pádraig a woeful teasing, however, saying that either he didn't know the difference between a peacock and a pheasant or else he was seeing things that weren't there. But he made us eat our words, when, less than an hour later, he called us out again and there the bird was, quite content-edly eating the bits of the bread Pádraig was throwing to it, the rainbow of colours on its neck glistening in the sunlight as it practically took the bread from his hand.

How I wanted it! But, shortly after, as we all debated what to do about getting it to stay, it took flight and, spreading its wings, glided gracefully over the garden wall. We all rushed down then, and out onto the road. But not a trace of it could be seen, no matter how we searched. It had apparently melted into thin air. So, resigning myself to the inevitable, I went back in home and swore that this time I really was going to go the proper way about buying myself a peacock or two.

Then, later that day, when I was doing some washing in the sink, didn't I see our visiting peacock in the back yard eating what the dogs had left over after their dinner. I sup-plemented this with hastily thrown bits of bread, and even with some perfectly fresh, sweet cake. It stayed around until dark and then flew up into a nearby tree.

We were all like children, looking up the tree in the morning to see if our visitor was still around. And sure enough, it was, in all its finery, and it graciously accepted our breakfast offerings. The sons then begged some meal from a poultry-rearing neighbour. It condescended to eat that too and seemingly settled in for the day. I kept checking every so often and I never went out empty-handed.

At one stage, as I pegged out the clothes, it gave me quite a fright, however, by suddenly giving the most extraordinary cry right behind me. It transpired that it was looking for some more food from me because it is inclined to play that trick ever since. It loves chips, we found, but hates baked beans. It goes clear crazy for anything in the line of cake. I do believe it has a real sweet tooth. He, for we are nearly sure it is a male, admires himself greatly in the porch windows, prancing and pacing back and forth, cocking his head from side to side.

In other words, he has totally adopted us. His name is Charlie; his fine feathers, short mincing steps and his way of going reminding us forcibly of a certain gentleman. Now if somebody out there is missing a peacock — we just don't want to know about it. And, unless there's an even better cake-baker in that house, neither does Charlie. Also, we are about to get him two peahens, to keep him at home in the future. I finally answered an ad in the paper.

Spring is Sprung

Eoin, like a young fellow again, is taking such pleasure in his land and his animals, that he is a headline to me today. And, best of all, he wants me to share it, to come and take a walk with him, to see, not only his mare and foal, but what the grass situation is really like. He said he'll be back for me in a half an hour to do just that.

You see, he also said that the sons are making noises about leaving the milking cows out to grass for a few hours today and it isn't even March yet. So part of me — the conservative part — wants to say, 'Hey! Hold on a minute,

winter isn't over yet.' But I am as good as gold. I firmly
pulled my zip for the lip tightly shut because, after all, it is
now really none of my business when the cows go out to
grass. Eoin and I are no longer the ones making those kind
of decisions. If the lads say that ground conditions are suitable and that there is sufficient grass cover there, well, unless we have done our job of training them very badly, they
should know best. We trust them totally after all. Didn't we
hand over the total management of our farm, our life's
work, practically our life's blood, to them?

However, we are still a little like that fellow, who said
that the way to go was to 'trust but verify'. Eoin wants to
walk that first paddock himself, physically testing it with
the heel of his boot, before he will be satisfied that the
ground conditions are really right. But he also wants to do it
nice and quietly, without the sons seeing him. He does not
want to be seen checking up on them. That would be fatal.
With fathers and sons it is vital that, as early as possible, the
father lets himself be guided by the son. Thus, the son becomes the real head, the real boss. Otherwise, it just does not
work. There are no two ways about that. When you let go,
you let go. But that doesn't prevent you from keeping a
more than keen interest in all that is going on and putting in
your tuppence ha'penny's worth occasionally. Otherwise you
may as well pack up entirely and go and live in the town.

Anyway, sons, who know that the final decisions do rest
in their hands, usually have no problem with the occasional
input from the old folk, if it is constructive. They'd be damn
fools too if they didn't occasionally draw on the accumulated wisdom of a life time — that knowledge of local conditions and that network of connections which cannot be
handed over as easily as the farm. I have often heard Eoin
Óg here saying to his dad to get on to so-and-so please for
him, because his dad appears to carry more weight in that
corner than he himself does. 'What do you think, Dad?' is
another thing I have heard regularly over the years of the

transition of power from father to son.

That transitional phase is the period of the family cycle which begins when the potential farming successor begins his working life, and ends when his predecessor retires from the position of head boss man. This transitional phase usually includes a period of co-operation between generations, to facilitate the gradual shift of power. There is no difficulty in deciding when this shift of power begins. It starts not the day that the son first comes home to work, but the day that a parent no longer goes to call the son to get up for work. Then, and only then, is power shifting. Because power is not something that a parent hands on a plate to an heir, saying 'Here, take that.' Power must also be seized, by the new farmer taking more and more responsibility onto himself, or indeed herself, by making decisions — even the decision of when to get up in the morning.

The most dramatic decision made on this farm each year is when to go out to grass by day. In many ways it is the highlight, the turning point of the year, which I have never willingly missed. Everybody then smiles with pure pleasure at the antics of the cows high-tailing it on the farm road. Is there any happier sight than even the stately old matrons in the herd throwing their heels up in the air, just once more, and galloping off like the young ones? I love watching this each year, just as I do the first calf being born, and even the day that comes, usually in May, when Eoin comes in to tell me that at last he can hear the grass growing.

That warm, damp, luscious day hasn't come yet, but it will. That much we do know. All hopes for the year ahead are bright once more the day the cows go out to grass. But we try not to go out so soon that those hopes will inevitably be dashed by the cows being brought in again, if it pours rain and the forecast is poor. So it isn't a case of just opening the gate and letting them off.

That is why I know the transitional period between the generations ended here the year that the cows were left out

to grass without as much as a by your leave to either Eoin or
myself. The first we knew of it was when we were told they
were gone. That, if I remember rightly, was a bit of a shock
to our systems. It may even have been a trial of strength that
day. Because power is the ability to impose your will on
another, whether they like it or not.

Well, whatever about the cows, Eoin did decide himself
to let out his mare and foal as well. They are all his. Though,
with another foal due shortly, I did hear some comment the
other day about was it a flock of the things he was planning
to have here next!

The Smell of a Grandchild

My granddaughter Rebecca in Australia is a year old today,
and we have never seen her. You know, I never feel hard
done by that three of my sons are emigrants. They went
willingly, even eagerly, and they are all constantly in touch
with home ever since. It is on occasions like this, however,
that the hard facts of emigration hit me badly.

It seems all wrong, somehow, that the flesh of my flesh,
the blood of my blood, should be a living, walking, talking,
breathing, little girl, and I have never once held her in my
arms. We have lots of photographs all right, and those videos
that Michael took, a little bit every week of her life, since she
was born. So, we have literally watched her grow, on tape,
before our very eyes. But that is not the same thing as holding her warm flesh near ours, and experiencing her with all
of our senses: the look of her; the feel of her; the sound of
her; and, above all, the smell of her.

The one thing all the videos, photographs, letters and
phonecalls going can't give is the smell of a baby, a child, a
person. Smells are important. There is that much of the
animal still in us humans. All animals recognise each other

in a special way by smell. I treasure the smell of Michaella, except when she fills her nappy of course. But even that is all right to me in a way that strange children's dirty nappies are not. All my sons smell differently too, and it isn't just the different after-shaves they use. I can also smell Eoin from his pillow-case when I am dressing the bed. And he says that if I am gone from the bed in the morning, before he himself wakes up, he always rolls over into my side because it smells of me.

And what was it Helen Lucy Burke used to go on about, in the hotels and guesthouses she was vetting? She'd always take off the pillow case to smell if there was a male smell from the pillows themselves. That earned the proprietors a severe rebuke in her column, and rightly so too. We laughed when we read it at the time, but you know she was quite right. I have done precisely that myself on occasions since — and did not like it one little bit some of the peculiar whiffs that hit my nose.

Anyway, I have my own little pillow that I always use at home — a nice flat one that just suits me best. So, ever since reading that article, unless I forget it when packing, that pillow goes everywhere with me. With it, I settle into sleep grand, even in a strange bed. It's my comforter in my old age, just like small children get attached to a sheet, or an old toy, and no replacement object will do, because it never smells right to them. So I like my pillow — the feel and the smell of it — and nothing else will do. I also read somewhere that Tony O'Reilly always travels with his own pillow, wherever he goes. So I am in high-class company. That made me feel less foolish somehow.

But feeling foolish is something that disappears with the years, more or less. You begin to please yourself and only yourself and what others think doesn't matter greatly. I may cringe with embarrassment at the memory of things said or done when I literally still feel hot under the collar at the memory of some past faux pas. It took me a long, long time before I realised that, in all probability, nobody else gave my embarrassing moments a second thought. They were all mine, and everybody else was only concerned with what others were thinking of them. People are only centre stage in the dramas of their own lives. Everybody else is off-stage really, except for brief supporting roles. And then they are retired again to the wings, quite out of the spotlight of everybody else's consciousness.

For that granddaughter of ours, however, we are nowhere at all in her life, not even in the wings off stage. So, naturally enough, I wonder what she is really like now on her first birthday. They tell me she is almost walking and far bigger and brighter than the normal one year old. Now tell me, where did I hear that before? It has a familiar ring to it somehow. I think that I heard it from every parent that ever there was. I also blush to remember all the times I said it myself about my own brood.

I even remember a story being told of my own grandfather who died when I was a baby. He was a rate collector as well as a farmer. So, he travelled the country into all sorts of homes. He used to wonder regularly just where did all the geniuses disappear to, because every day he went out on his job, collecting the rates, he met fathers and mothers full of talk about how really exceptional their child was. Yet going back, as he did, to those houses, year after year, he never did figure out just where all those geniuses disappeared to, when they grew up. He never once met an adult genius in his life, he said. Yet every parent is certain their baby is one. Sure I, in my day, thought that Rebecca's father was a genius too! So it wasn't off the stones in Australia she licked it.

APRIL

Send the Fool Further

I must tell you what happened to my youngest son last year on Fools' day, and which I only heard about this week. It never ceases to amaze me how long sometimes it is before parents hear things. But eventually, by one means or another, I reckon we get to hear just about everything, if not from themselves in a weak moment, then from their friends or, better still, their friends' parents. Although I do assure you, regardless of what my gang seems to think, our children are not the sole topic of conversation when we parents happen to meet. It's just that occasionally an odd snippet happens to leak out.

That's how I heard about John in his last year at school. He happened to miss a Christian Doctrine class on 31 March. The teacher had, for some weeks, been organising debates on various subjects to try and stimulate both their interest and learning. When my son came back from his visit to the dentist his classmates told him that his name had been drawn to open the next day's debate. John was to be the speaker on one side and his friend Tom the opposition.

Not even when he heard the topic, 'Sex before marriage — is it a good thing?' and that he was for the motion, did my lad smell a rat. His turn really was due. But he did not fancy his topic at all. Knowing, however, that the priest in question was a stickler for discipline, he set to his task and

spent hours that night preparing and trying to weasel out of
Tom what he was planning to say in rebuttal.

Tom would come out with only the craziest notions, and
since that son of mine dearly loves to win, no matter what
he turns his hand to, he really worked out a strong case for
sex before marriage. Then, next day, when their priest
teacher asked who was opening the debate, a unified roar
went up of 'John Kavanagh, Father.' Quite innocently, John,
who does happen to have the gift of the gab, went with his
friend Joe out to the front of the class and started off his
speech.

Now I didn't hear quite how far he got, or even what he
said, but I don't have to know in order to picture the scene.
And I doubt if some twenty boys of seventeen, sitting quietly
in their desks, could contain themselves long enough to let
the joke proceed to the bitter end. Some one of them must
have broken ranks before John had time to hang himself
completely. One of them would be unable to stop himself
shouting out 'April fool, John!' and bringing the whole
proceedings to an uproarious end. I did not hear much of
their teacher's reaction either. But I do strongly suspect that
he was quite aware of what was happening and decided to
play along as well.

John still will not talk to me of that day. Yet, no matter
how mortified he felt at the time, he is bound to tell that
yarn over and over in adulthood. He will be able to laugh at
it too, by then, because there was no personal malice involved. He was chosen to be the butt of the joke only because he was the only one to have missed their Christian
Doctrine class the day before.

The only April Fool jokes I really can tolerate are the
clever ones and not just the 'send the fool further' ones that
are the usual run of the mill. I can never see the point of
calling people for non-existent phone calls and that sort of
thing.

The Water Pump and the Sledge-hammer

Eoin has never been known for his mechanical genius and that's for sure. He and the combustion engine do not have a good relationship. His relationship with tools is even worse. It is so bad that I swear tools in this place go and hide deliberately on him.

Well, they certainly go AWOL. Whenever a wheel had to be taken off because of a bad puncture, you could always be quite sure that the exact size of socket needed was always the very one missing from the socket box — that is, provided that the box could be found in the first place! Nobody, but nobody, ever then remembers who had it last. You see, when a repair job is going badly here, there is a certain propensity for tools to fly through the air, to land God knows where, with a litany of suitable curses following them. So, can you really blame any tool that goes AWOL on this farm?

Some years ago, at a farm discussion group walk, they all were taken into the toolshed of the owner who really is a mechanical genius. Now, here there really was a space for everything and everything was in its place. Each tool even had its outline drawn on the wall, so any missing item was immediately obvious. All the group were mightily impressed, and said so, as did Eoin. But then Eoin added that he himself had spent most of that very morning looking for a vicegrip until finally he had to give up and go down to the co-op stores to buy a new one. The contrast between the two extremes, of perfection and chaos, was so strong that all the men there thought it the funniest thing they had ever heard, possibly because in the continuum between perfection and chaos they may have figured somewhere nearer Eoin's end of the line, but wouldn't come straight out and admit it, like my fellow.

But if they thought that was funny — Eoin having to go

and buy a new vicegrip simply because he couldn't find any
of the several that should be around — they should have
seen him the famous morning he wanted to take a sledge
hammer to a petrol-driven water pump. When Eoin first
had marriage in mind, he had got a petrol-driven pump,
with a pull start, so that the toilet would flush and the water
run in the taps. Before that, all these things would depend
on whether there was enough rain, or not, to fill the tanks
from the water falling on the roofs. Otherwise, water was
brought in buckets from that shallow well in the yard

I suffered quite a culture shock when I first married and
came to a home without electricity. Visiting beforehand, I
thought the soft, gentle light of the oil lamps, coupled with
the great roaring fires, was so romantic. However, I quickly
found out the disadvantages of filling paraffin lamps every
morning and the impossibility of getting Aladdin lamps to
stay lighting properly. The mantle was forever blackening,
no matter what I did. So, if on my own, I regularly had to
stop whatever I was doing, to turn the flame low to burn off
the black. There often wasn't even a radio to listen to if the
batteries had run out and, of course, my collection of records
stayed at home after me.

But, it is really in connection with the farm that it is more
important to play the game of 'I remember, I remember', to
show the modern generation just why farming could not
progress in any area before the coming of rural electrifica-
tion. How many cows would they, or could they, now milk
by hand, or draw water for, in 1996?

It is only when the electricity fails, for one reason or another, that everybody gets a little taste of past times, which
is no great harm at all to them. We had it tough in those
years, trying to calve or milk cows, or help sows farrow,
with nothing but storm lanterns for light. The tilly lamp came
later, which worked under pressure and gave a tremendous
light. But I never knew a household with more than one of
those, and, anyway, it was usually the sole property of the

man of the house, to be used only at his discretion. I also remember the storm lanterns, which, when I was a child, had to light up the stall at my old home for winter milkings when ten cows per milker was considered good.

Thus, twice in my lifetime I saw the coming of electricity to an area. It came to my old home in the late 1940s. But it was 1962 before we finally got electricity here. And I do know that there are pockets of the country where it was even later. So we, and those like us, had a very short period of time to build up a herd before milk quotas struck. Our first herd of cows, all eight of them, were milked by a Lister portable milking machine, when that too would start. Otherwise it was out with the bucket and three-legged stool, plus a good spancel for those Eoin went to milk. He was never reared to hand-milking like I was.

Still, what I remember most from those years was the water situation. On my first visit to my future home I cheerfully used the bathroom, twice. It was afterwards I discovered that before this official visit poor Eoin had spent ages up and down the ladder with buckets of water to fill the tank over the bathroom. That day, of all days, he couldn't get the petrol water pump in the yard well to start. I had wondered all right about the function of a white enamel water bucket, with a lid, near the loo. I later discovered another such bucket in the kitchen beside the sink.

It was many the time I myself went to that well to fill those buckets in the years that followed, purely because that petrol engine was the most cantankerous thing imaginable. Some days it would fire grand, after one or two pulls. But, more often, I thought that Eoin — young man and all that he was at the time — would get a heart attack, or at the very least burst a blood vessel, as he endlessly pulled on that start rope. And he'd get madder and madder and more and more vocal as not a kick could be got out of the engine and he knew he was facing a trip into the city, once more, to have the damn thing repaired.

Eoin did so hate to see me drawing buckets of water. I think this was because he felt he had let me down somehow, bringing me to a place without even running water in the house. And, while drawing water was then expected of most rural women, this was not going to happen to his wife. God love him, but he could have drawn dozens of buckets — all the water I could possibly need — with the energy he wasted on that pump when it refused to start.

That same well had eels living in it, which you could easily see in the clear water before the first bucket was dipped. How they got into it was always a mystery to me in those days before television explained all such marvels. All we knew then was that the overflow from the well fed the horses' pond. Only, if there was any overflow from that, it went out, via a drain, onto the roadside. It was years later, early one morning, that we found a huge eel four fields away from the well, dragging itself along the wet grass trying to find its way, I suppose, to the river. We couldn't begin to imagine how it had got out of the well in the first place. I now know that the little elvers returning from the Sargasso sea had enough water in the roadside drains to find their way back. But not one of those did I ever see.

The first time I saw an eel close up was when I inadvertently caught one in a bucket of water. Innocently, I brought the bucket — eel and all — into the house, in wonderment. I was sent back out, quickly, with the full bucket of water, because to bring in an eel like that was considered extremely unlucky. The well would now almost certainly go dry as a result of my ignorance. The luck would also go from the house, and where would we all be then? Of course, I now know that the only reason my dipping bucket brought up the eel was that the water had already run very low anyway, so the prophecy of a dry well, which did actually happen that year, was, even then, well on its way to fulfilment. But those were much more innocent times for me as well as everybody else.

Anyway, each time that petrol pump drove Eoin past the point of frustration, into a temper outburst, he swore that the very first time he got an electric pump installed, he was going to take a sledge hammer, and, with the utmost satisfaction, make absolute bits of that torment of his existence — which was precisely what he planned once it was truly and finally redundant. That pump, when the new electric one was installed and proved to be working, was, with all due ceremony, placed in the middle of the yard, outside the back door. I was there to bear witness. However, there then arose one slight hitch. Eoin just could not find his sledge hammer, wherever it had gone and hidden itself. So the pump-smashing ceremony just had to wait. But it did get a good hard kick as a foretaste of things to come.

A Bit of a Balls

I am sleeping alone these nights and I don't like it one little bit. There is great comfort to wake in the night and feel a warm body there beside one, even if I do at times envy Eoin his happy state of being sound asleep while I toss and turn. Broken sleep patterns unfortunately follow depression. And, if things are just too awful and selfishness takes over, just to be held helps.

This week, however, I am in a very serious frame of mind. Eoin is in hospital, having had a lump removed from a testicle. There now, that wasn't too hard to say, was it, even though everyone, especially men, seem to shy totally away from even the mention of such a subject? One man, with whom I was my usual direct self when we met during the week, confessed that he personally had told everyone he was operated on for his back when he had the exact same job done on him some years ago. That was to explain his bow-legged walk when he got on his feet again. As a total aside, isn't it extraordinary how, when you have a problem yourself, you suddenly meet, or hear of, others all over the place with exactly the same complaint?

I have also had a few irate friends on the phone to me these past few days, giving out that they never knew about Eoin, and why hadn't the sons told them, and they only speaking to one or other of them during the week? Or why hadn't I myself picked up the phone to tell them? The answer to the second question is dead simple. There is no way I could phone anybody up and say, 'Hey listen! Eoin is in hospital.' That would be tantamount to putting the gun to their heads and saying they must go and visit him there. And, of course, since people never go hospital visiting empty-handed, they would then feel obliged to go shopping first as well, to make matters even worse. As for the first question — why my sons were unusually silent about their father's condition — I honestly don't know the answer to that one.

I suspect, however, that it was that particular portion of their father's anatomy that caused their unusual taciturnity. One son actually said that he wasn't sure which was the greatest shock to him — to find out that his father had a possible malignancy or to discover that the pair of us old fogies were still sexually active. You see it was I who found the lump. Eoin, the wretch, knew he had it for quite some weeks, but thought it would go away, didn't want to worry me, and so on.

Now, this is where I am going to get deadly serious, with men of all ages. A young man, a friend of my sons, desperately wanted to do medicine. So he worked heroically hard all his Leaving Cert year to get those elusive points. But he was foolhardy in the extreme because, before the Christmas of that year, he knew he had a testicular lump. He, however, told nobody at all about it until the very day he finished his final exam in the summer. Then, and only then, he told his father, who is a doctor.

Suffice it to say that things moved pretty quickly then. By the time the Leaving Cert results came out — and this boy had enough points to do anything he wanted in any college in Ireland — he and his family were also facing up to the fact that his lump was cancerous, treatment was on-going and the future was uncertain, to say the least. The same lad went to college, his ambition achieved. But he was dead before his Pre-Med results came out the following summer. Tragically he had again got honours overall, despite his illness and somewhat erratic attendance at lectures before his final exams.

Now, this is by no means the only story I know about young men and testicular cancer. A happier one is of a New Zealander, here in Ireland, who told his host one morning of his 'little problem'. He was operated on, fast and very successfully. The extraordinary follow-up to that story is that no less that three of his cohorts, from that same valley in New Zealand, also developed the same disease. Unfortunately, none of these survived. Therefore, there is one family in New Zealand eternally grateful both to Irish medicine and that one particular host family who made their young visitor's problem their problem. But that young man also opened his mouth in time.

This knowledge — that testicular cancer is normally a young man's disease — was, however, my great consolation with my discovery of Eoin's lump. His doctor, while looking serious at the recital of symptoms, on examination said that he was almost sure the lump was benign. Still, Eoin was to go at once to a specialist — a urologist — and was also to have an immediate ultrasound done. Each of these events proved reassuring. But he was told that surgery was necessary and, with me anyway, the fear of the worst lingered, despite all reassurances to the contrary, until the final verdict came from the laboratory.

I can't begin to tell you of our relief when the doctor came round, the day after the operation, examined his handiwork, and then, almost as a throwaway remark, said that the test had come back negative, as expected. And you know, until then, neither of us had let on to the other that we both had those lingering doubts despite all the expert opinion already given. Then Eoin began to joke that in future he would have much more sympathy for any bullocks having the job done on them. There would be no more castration at a late stage on our farm anyway.

In fact, from that moment on, Eoin has quite enjoyed his little stay in hospital, apart from the pain and discomfort, of course. And why wouldn't he with all those pretty young nurses dancing attendance on him day and night? And that, even though he has not even once rung his bell — he is the kind of man who would put up with anything rather than cause trouble. But the other day this young nurse came in to find out what he needed — why had he rung his bell? Eoin got quite flustered and apologetic, saying it must have been hit accidentally. When she was back again a few minutes later, again to answer his call, we discovered it was our two granddaughters who were exploring the bathroom very thoroughly indeed!

Well, it was better that than jumping on top of their grandfather in the bed because, when we arrived in, he was lying back in the bed, suffering, as he said, 'not only like a castrated bullock, but also like a stuffed pig'. This was the result of his five-course lunch. I knew then that he was well on the mend again and I won't be sleeping alone very much longer. But I'll never be able to keep up the five-course lunches and that's for sure, whatever about the dancing attendance on him.

Farming Wives

Eoin came in to me this evening a very happy man indeed. And I'll tell you why. He had been up to see his son, Pádraig, and met his daughter-in-law in the yard. She was just about to go for the cows with his two granddaughters. They, in the meantime, were having the greatest of fun cycling up and down the milking parlour. Michaella now is cycling perfectly. She showed her grandfather, with great pride, how the safety wheels are off her bicycle at long last. That has been her ambition now for quite some time.

'Daddy said that I was no longer making noise with them on the ground. So he took them off. Now I can go way faster....' she explained, very seriously. And off she went to demonstrate that very fact, down one side of their new parlour, out the collecting yard and back in again the other side. Nicole, bless her, plodded along after her, as quickly as her plump little legs would pedal her tricycle. Both of them loved the audience and the plentiful words of praise they got for their efforts. But then, don't we all?

Eoin then went for the cows himself, with Michaella proudly telling him how to open and shut the wires to the paddock. It was all 'My daddy does this' and 'My mammy does that' with her, Eoin drawing her out without a doubt. Sara had stayed back to get the milking parlour ready. And, as Eoin closed the gate into the collection yard, there she was, starting in already to milk her cows — to the manner born — while waiting for Pádraig to finish spreading nitrogen on the paddock the cows had just come off.

The girls, quite happily, went up to their room over the dairy to continue their play, and to show their grandfather all their things up there. He had a tea party with the dolls while enjoying his bird's eye view of the milking going on below through the viewing window. The girls are very secure up there, since they can check regularly on their parents and their parents on them. Michaella even uses the desk there to do her lessons. So Eoin finished up doing sums and helping her to write out three sentences with the word 'hide' in them.

Then, having escaped, Eoin came back home, to find his other daughter-in-law milking the cows here, with her husband. He could hear the chat between them before he ever set foot in the milking parlour. So, he backed out again before they were even aware of his presence. Anyway, he was bursting to come in and tell me of our blessedness. 'Both lots of them reminded me so much of us, when we were their age,' he concluded, as if that was the supreme accolade.

Now, all that may seem to be such a small thing to have delighted Eoin quite so much, or for me to write about. Indeed, I have no doubt at all that some people are already thinking that the two young wives — city reared — should not be so involved in farm work at all, that there is no need for it surely ... the rest you can fill in for yourself!

I wonder, however, if anybody has ever passed such re-marks to their face. I must ask both lots some time, and find out how they felt if it did happen. I know that I was once asked, thirty or more years ago, if I wasn't ashamed of my life 'hawking eggs and vegetables into town'. It was a seri-ous question too, not a rhetorical one posed in anger. That is why the words stuck so firmly in my memory, even though, fortunately, I was able to give a quick answer at the time. I soon told that farmer's wife that any 'hawking' I was doing paid me real well.

Then, when there wasn't much talk of women's rights, I wonder would I have got more upset by the remark if the financial reward at the time wasn't quite so visible in the heel of my fist? We were growing cauliflowers for the Sugar Company that year. The price we got for them was less than two old pence per head, and, for that princely sum they had to be totally cut down to the mere head itself, and delivered, in special boxes, to the nearest railway station.

However, the crop was absolutely massive, in every sense of the word. That seed, supplied by the company, was really good. It had an excellent germination rate. So we planted out more acres than we had contracted to do. Every plant then headed into the most colossal size I have ever seen in cauliflowers. We were calculating our profits as they headed out. But then the Sugar Company would not take even all the crop specified in the contract.

Eoin then went looking for a market and found a whole-saler who would take all we had at the time, at eight pence a head, with no fiddly preparation work either. All we had to do was deliver them in by the car-trailer load. That was when I became adept at backing a car trailer, since I was heavily pregnant at the time and less well able to bend to cut the next load. We were really busy because another buyer collected them here, in the yard, at sixpence a head. So there was no contest. Contract or not, all the cauliflowers went to where there was the demand and the price was best.

And yes, since we did have hens on deep litter at the time, in the old grain lofts, I also carried in boxes of eggs, twice a week at least, to the man with the milk round who bought them from us. And no, I was not ashamed to do any of that, because, quite bluntly, we badly needed the money. And, like our two families farming today, we were in this thing together. I also got paid for each load on the spot, There was no blooming paper work following every trans-action then, for us or our buyers.

With hindsight, however, what I now realise is that I was being confronted with the idea, just then becoming very prevalent indeed in the Ireland of the 1960s, that it was somehow undignified for women to become involved in farmwork that was really the province of men. Farmers' wives, emerging from the hungry decades, the 1940s and the 1950s, were then in the process of becoming just 'housewives' who happened to live on farms. I was letting down the side, in other words, not being quite the 'lady'.

On the other hand, men, being the contradictory crea-
tures they are, have much more value on the woman who is
actively involved in farm work, than on the woman who
works twice as hard inside the house, polishing, dusting
under the beds, endlessly cooking or whatever.

However, there was always just one important proviso. It
was all right for a woman to work on the farm, just so long
as she was seen to be just helping her husband. This was a
thin line beyond which a woman really should not go. For
example, it was quite all right for me to cut the cauliflowers
in the field, and to prepare them for market, heavily pregnant or not. But going to the market myself — that was not a
done thing. That was a male prerogative, regardless.

Once, when a childless wife was the one who went into
the auctioneer's box at the Mart, to sell the store cattle, even
though her husband was also there, it occasioned mutterings and jeering comments of how it would be fitter for her
to be at home with half a dozen children. Later that night, in
the pub, a local wag was heard to remark that 'Johnny
would be a grand fellow all right — if it wasn't for that man
he married....' Which leads me to wonder was the same ever
said about Eoin!

MAY

The Confirmation Class of '77

I must be getting soft in my old age because I find that, now, I often drive the youngest to and from school. The rest of them were made to go under their own steam — shank's mare or bicycles, the choice was theirs. I felt that both they and I were all the better for their getting themselves to school. They did say, however, when they wanted to make me feel guilty, that they were the only ones in the parish who had to get their own lunches because I was never in from the cows in time.

Be that as it may, like me in my day, the best fun was always that to be had on the way home from school. Great was the devilment that took place from time to time. Half the things that happened, the parents never got to hear a word about. This, of course, is just as well. Occasionally, however, with my lot anyway, outside forces came into play and we were made only too well aware of what went on as they made their leisurely way home from school.

I still get hot under the collar when I remember what my two youngest got up to this time last year. There were quite a few repercussions after that little escapade of theirs and that's for sure. Anyway, it was on a fine May day, just like today, that they were dead late getting home to their dinner. They had kept me from the garden as I waited for them. Whatever about the mornings, I did always try to be in when they got home from school, because they always seemed to need that time to tell me about their day and to hear themselves what had been happening at home in their absence.

I was in little humour for a long chat this day, however. So they got their dinner slapped up in front of them with cross inquiries about what had kept them so long. I was hardly waiting for the answer as I pulled on my gardening gloves. But my youngest put a quick halt to my gallop out to the garden.

'We were up to the parish priest to complain the Master, Mammy,' he blurted out, all red in the face and close enough to tears. My face must have shown my shock and disbelief because before I could draw breath, Pádraig quickly re-assured me.

'It's all right, Mammy. He wasn't a bit cross with us. He laughed a lot, gave us lemonade and biscuits and said we were great little men....'

You can be sure I left my garden after me on the spot as I sat down at the table to ferret the whole story out of them. I was hoping against hope that the facts of the case were not as bad as that first bald statement of Eoin Óg's had inti-mated. It was though, and indeed it proved worse when I got the full story.

It seemed the Master had been crosser than usual, it be-ing Confirmation time, with all the headaches that implied for the poor man. The Bishop was due at the school that week and the teacher was trying to hammer the catechism into the Confirmation class. My two ruffians were confirmed together last year because the Bishop only comes to this parish every second year for Confirmations. And, while they no longer are examined in their Christian Doctrine in front of everybody in the church, as was done in my day, I sometimes think the examination in the school is even more stressful for children. In the church, with everybody all dressed up, one can hardly be refused Confirmation.

Although, as Eoin can testify, that's not strictly true. When he was making his Confirmation, even longer ago than my day, one little girl was turned away at the altar when she missed two questions from the Bishop. Eoin said that he never did get over the fright of then waiting for his turn to be examined after watching that poor misfortunate girl, in her white dress and veil, having to get up from her place at the altar rails and walk back down the centre aisle to where her parents were kneeling. Eoin remembers that he was asked to say the Creed and to name two of the seven deadly sins. And he knew them too, in spite of his terror, because, as he says, they were bet into him at school.

In spite of all that, there is still no doubt that he and his Confirmation classmates, in those different times, would never have done what my sons' classmates did last year. Didn't the whole lot of them, on the road home, decide to go up to the parish priest whose house they had to pass, in order to complain the Master about all the slaps they had got that day.

'After all, Mammy, Johnny Stack says that his daddy told him that the Master is no longer allowed to slap us if we don't know our lessons. It's against the law now. He is only allowed to slap us if we are bold,' gabbled Eoin Óg, obviously repeating somebody else's words 'And we all got slapped today for not knowing our Catechism. So Johnny said that the parish priest was the only man who could stop the Master slapping us,' he concluded, the tears welling again, whether in remembrance of the pain of the slaps or else with the stress of my cross-questioning.

Of course, there is always a Johnny Stack, or his equivalent, in every group — the one who knows it all, and what should be done about it as well. So, with him as ringleader, they decided that he, my two sons, and a couple of the girls were to form the deputation. All the others — the more timid or else the wiser children — decided they wouldn't go in to the parochial house but would wait outside in the garden, in order to determine the outcome.

'Cowards they all were in the end,' said Pádraig disdain-
fully. 'Most of them never got even as far as his garden.
They stayed down at the gate. More of them, even Johnny
too, stayed outside....' and he went on to tell me how in the
finish there were only the two of them left and he had to lift
Eoin Óg up so as to reach the door bell. I could easily picture
the scene with my two bucks steeling their courage as they
waited for an answer. As luck would have it the parish
priest himself answered the door, so they were able to spill
out their tale of woe, on the doorstep, before their courage
forsook them.

'And I told him all about the others down at the gate and
just outside in the garden,' said Eoin Óg. 'And he looked
down and laughed out loud when they ducked into the
bushes as he came outside the porch to look.'

'Did he know who you were?' I then asked, hopefully.
But my hopes were quickly dashed. 'Oh yes, Mammy,' they
both answered at once, and with some pride. 'He said
"Aren't you the young Kavanaghs?"'

Resigned to the inevitable, I then listened to the rest of
their story. They told me how they had been taken in for
'chocolate biscuits and fizzy lemonade', the height of perfection in their eyes, and that they had told the priest all
about their teacher and their school.

Eoin had come into the kitchen by this stage. So I got
them to tell their whole story, all over again. from the beginning. There wasn't, however, the reaction I'd expected
from their father. He seemed to think it was the funniest
thing he had heard in a long time. So, the telling became
embellished with more and more little details under his
encouragement, to the obvious delight of his sons. I would
say it was just the kind of thing Eoin wished he had had the
courage to do in his own schooldays. I had severe reserva-
tions about the whole episode, however. But still I hoped
against hope that it would now die a natural death and

there'd be no more about it once I'd wiped the delighted grin off Eoin's face.

My fears were well founded, however. The pair were home from school, on time, the next day, with both of them practically in tears this time. All the bravado of the day before was completely gone. With no urging on my part, it all came rushing out this time.

'The Master said, when the priest was gone, that we were mean dirty sneaks, Mammy ... But he didn't say a word at all to the rest of them and they were there too....'

I jumped in fast. 'What do you mean "when the priest was gone"?' The answer I got sent me straight to the phone to try to straighten the whole matter out.

I got onto the PP first of all. He got quite defensive and said he felt it was his duty to act on the children's complaints. 'They were such a polite pair of boys too,' he concluded, in an attempt, I think, to soften my distress. But I knew that didn't matter a damn because my sons had to finish out their time in that school and I didn't want any ill-will towards them to develop. I personally had suffered enough from one particular teacher who had it in for me with much less cause.

So, my next, and more difficult, call was to the teacher. He said that he thought that Eoin and I had been behind the complaint and had encouraged our sons to do what they did. In the end, I finished up explaining to both teacher and priest that it was only a childish prank and that we had no complaints. (I lacked the courage of my sons when it came to the sticking point.)

Eventually, after a few days, all was smoothed over. But my two sons learned a very valuable lesson in life. They will know now that to be the spokesman, or leader, of any group, is a thankless job. It is a much wiser thing to lead from behind, as Johnny Stack did that day from the bushes.

The Way We Were

Isn't there something quite magical about these evenings? Everything is positively pulsating with new life. My calves are at last off my hands: they are out on grass, galloping and jumping all over the place with the sheer pleasure of life. They just love being out in the sunshine with, of course, all that luscious green grass to eat. But most of all they love their new-found freedom.

Freedom — what a lovely thought. Wouldn't I just love the freedom to do precisely what I wanted all day long? Ah well, at least these long evenings are mine — all mine — to spend in the garden. That special May evening light throws strange deep shadows and gives an unreal beauty to the most mundane groupings of plants. Even the weeds are beautiful in their own way even if it is because they too are at the peak of their mad May gallop, and growing apace. The sap is rising in all living things. Indeed, a little of it is inclined to rise in Eoin and myself, as well, betimes.

Every evening, after the supper, I can be contented all by myself — weeding, planting, staking, sowing still more seeds, with only the onset of darkness driving me indoors. Nothing else — not even the midges — can do that. Eoin is tempted out some evenings too, by the beauty of this time of the year, even though he says it is his conscience does it. 'How could you expect me to sit down and watch television,' he plaintively asks, tweaking my conscience in turn, 'with you out here working away until dark?'

But I know there is more to it than that. He feels the lure too — the powerful attraction of the May growth. He usually works with me in the garden a while, in companionable silence, or else chatting away. And I know quite well that, sooner rather than later, his talk will turn to how the barley is growing, to wondering are the new grass seeds up yet, plus, of course, the perennial question of how much grass there is in front of the cows.

Then he'll ask if I wouldn't leave that old weeding after me and come for a walk with him? And I do always go with him, with, I hope, not much more than a wistful look back at my lupins. I know I would just hate it were the day to come when he stopped asking me to go with him. I get a great sense of togetherness as we go, usually hand in hand, across the fields. And sometimes we stop a while if it is a really fine night. I did tell you that the sap rises in us too this time of the year. And is there any other way of life that a husband and wife can share quite so fully as farming?

I feel quite sorry for those farm women who boast that they never set foot outside their own back door. They seem to me to be wilfully closing that door on all sorts of richness and fulfilment. And one does not really have to know all that much about farming to participate in the ritual of walking the land. It is just a case of being there with them whether or not the right noises are made in the right places. Our men do need us for much more than as childminders, bed-mates or even food providers. They get much more out of the fact that you walked with them on a fine May evening, than the fact that you baked a fancy cake for their late supper. Yet both things take much the same time to do.

I personally get great satisfaction in standing in the middle of the cows, who, at long last, have their bellies full of food. It is such a relief after the tough time we went through this spring when we were afraid that they'd have nothing to eat but the bare concrete, when the back walls of the silage pit came perilously quickly into sight, and still the rain didn't stop. From the day they went out, our cows were chasing after every blade of grass that grew. It came to the stage that, on the second round, we'd give the cows their ration for the day and didn't dare go near them again until milking time. There'd have been a stampede if they even saw us in the distance, not to mind to have anyone walk into the field to them. As it was, you'd hear them roaring across country, betimes.

Now, at last, all that is behind us and the cows are too full and contented even to budge at our coming. They stay there, grazing leisurely or just ruminating and more or less ignoring us. Only the odd curious one may come up behind us to take a tug at our clothing, like a child looking for attention.

I was reading somewhere recently that the 'flight distance' of cows is twelve feet. 'Flight distance' was explained as the distance between man and cow before the cow moves away. The better the stock-man, the smaller the distance. So I take great delight in the fact that 'my' cows, because I milk them more often than Eoin does, come right up to us. The article said that a herd with a flight distance of three to zero feet is cared for by a very good stockman indeed.

Next time I am at a farm walk, or just seeing cows somewhere else, I must take note of their flight distance and then draw my own conclusions. I must also take note of how the cows behave when our farming son is in the field with our cows. I have a strong suspicion that he is just that little bit too free with his fist, or the stick, when he is milking. Personally I would ban all sticks from the milking parlour. Whenever any of my menfolk are doing the milking, however, there is always a stick left after them, even though they tell me that they were just used to 'hurry up' the cows on their way in for milking. And then they wonder why they get kicked in the milking parlour — cows are no fools, you know.

Thinking of fine May evenings always reminds me as well of a sister of Eoin's who was pestered by one particular man to go out with him. Time after time, she refused him, and still the fool came back, again and again, to ask her for a date. Finally, fed up with his attentions, and purely to shut him up, she said that she would go out with him — the first fine day in May. It was sometime around Christmas she made that promise, and she often repeated it in the months that followed. But, of course, that fine enough day in May never came, either that year or any other year either.

So, no matter what month it is, don't just promise to walk the land with your man the first fine day in May. Do it when he asks. You'd never know what it might lead to out there, away from everyone and everything, except perhaps the curious cows with a low flight distance.

A Time of Promise

May is by far and away my favourite month of the year — with everything so full of life and the hope of still better to come. It is just like the glorious springtime of life. Yet how tragically often the promise is so much better than the fulfilment.

None of the farm or garden crops are mature yet, so we are fully justified in expecting bumper yields of just about everything. My young folk too, in their springtime of life, rightly expect life to be always kind and fruitful for them. Too well you and I know that the potatoes can get blighted, there may still be a late frost to kill off the young fruitlets, the grass may shrivel and brown in drought, the corn may lodge and be unmillable, and the summer may yet prove wet and cold.

Right now, that is impossible to believe. My garden is a riot of colour. My vegetables are growing apace. Eoin is smiling again with the spectre of hunger for his cows long gone. Last night he pulled me out of the garden once more to go for a walk with him. He said that if we but stood in any field, we could, at last, hear the grass growing. I was tempted to tell him that he need only stand near me and we'd both hear the weeds growing.

I wage an endless war on weeds. And if I was to cease my warfare for any few days, they'd get the better of me and

take over. Gardening is really an outdoor housekeeping job
of endlessly tidying up. The house isn't too bad at the moment because, with the boys still at school, what I do stays
done. But, once they set foot inside the door, I have to start
picking up after them all over again. It is a case of one shoe
here and its companion God knows where. Socks are lost in
the beds or to be found behind cushions or draped over the
banister. Skateboards are usually left where Eoin is most
likely to fall over them. Worst of all, however, are the mugs,
plates and bits of food left in the oddest places, where
they've had their snacks between meals. I'm the sorry
woman I didn't get glass tops for all my tables before they
got so hopelessly ringed by hot coffee mugs.

Honestly, is there any end to what teenage boys eat at
this active time of the year? I sometimes swear that my lot
must have hollow legs to hold all they pack away in a
twenty-four-hour period. But wouldn't it be far worse, to be
paying doctors' bills for them? I said to myself as I squir-
reled away yet more cakes into the freezer against the imminent return of my non-exam ones. Seamus, our second
son, is doing his Leaving Cert this year, and only dying for
the day it is all over and he comes farming full-time with
Eoin. The last Sunday he was home I was full of sympathy
for him with the stress of the exam coming on him so soon.
He only laughed in my face, however, and said it would be a
'push-over' for him. I only hope he is right, although he
could do with some of the cockiness knocked out of him.

I still get sad when I think of how my eldest fretted and
worried before, during, and after his Leaving Cert last year.
It just doesn't seem fair that Seamus will probably come
through with flying colours, even if by no means at his full
potential, when poor old Michael was the one who worked
so hard. I know, however, that there was more rejoicing over
every pass mark Michael got than any honours this fellow
may yet achieve without even trying.

It bothers me a little sometimes that the mere fact that

Seamus decided on farming as a career so long ago meant that he never gave his full attention to his studies. I have a sneaking suspicion that his teachers didn't concentrate particularly on him either, in class, because he left everybody in no doubt that he was going to be a farmer. The general expectation still is that farmers don't really need all that much education to succeed, and that bothers me.

I'll never forget our visit to one of the most prestigious boarding schools in Ireland when we interviewed them about our sons' education. Our third son was only a few months old when we took the daft notion of booking them into a whole lot of different schools on the premise that we had no idea what they would be like, or more pertinently, what we'd be able to afford, when they got to boarding school stage. We were not thinking then of having five of them in the one school at one and the same time, of course, or we would never have driven our second-hand car up that long and imposing avenue.

Having stated our business, we were interviewed in a book-lined room, by a Fr Crow, who sat on the other side of a broad mahogany desk. All was going swimmingly until Eoin made his fatal mistake. Fr Crow asked him what did he plan his sons would do in life. Eoin's immediate reply was that he hoped as many of them as possible would go farming. At this, Fr Crow stood up, obviously ending the interview with these decisive words: 'I suggest, with all due respect, Mr Kavanagh, if you want your sons to follow you into agriculture that you send them elsewhere. Here we educate for medicine, the sciences and the law.' He finished by putting out his hand for Eoin to shake.

The man was lucky he was still behind that broad desk because I have rarely seen Eoin so mad. He took as a personal insult the inference that farmers were not considered good enough for that school. We went back down that broad avenue with a swirl of gravel and Eoin swearing that no son of his would ever be sent there, no matter what.

Of course, as events transpired, we could never have afforded to send all five of them to that college anyway. Also, all these years later, especially when Seamus said that about his Leaving Cert being a 'push-over', it crossed my mind that that 'terrible Fr Crow', as Eoin still terms him, was really wiser than we appreciated. If we had sent that son of ours there, he probably would have no notion of becoming a farmer now. The pressure from above, as well as the peer pressure, would have insured that his feet were put on a different track entirely. That same lad has bags of ability and is also extremely competitive.

As it is, he is not a bit pushed since he is the envy of many of the boys in the school he is at, because he has a farm to come home to — their parents sent them to boarding school in the first place in order to give them a way out of farming. Anyway, that decision was made long ago, to send him where he went, and there is no point now in asking, 'What if?'

Now we are back to decision time once again as we wonder what is the best training for young farmers these days. There seem to be conflicting opinions on that subject. Some tell us to be sure to send him to an agricultural college for a year to learn his trade. Others then tell us that he would be better off spending a year at home first, to learn the practical ins and outs of farming. That seems a pretty sensible approach to me at the moment, and, God knows, Eoin could do with a strong young man about the place.

But therein lies another danger. It would be so very easy to become dependent on Seamus. After all, that was our prime motive in choosing boarding school for our sons — so that their studies could come first. If they had been at home, it goes without saying that they would have been called out to help when any little emergency arose on the farm.

So, even on this lovely May evening, there are decisions to be pondered. But I'm hoping that there will be a long, glorious Summer between now and the real decision time in

September. I always get nervous when I can see no clear-cut answer to a question. The 'what if?'s are always inclined to come back to haunt us. There is always some regret for the path not taken.

From Birthdays to Afterbirths

My granddaughter Nicole was one year old this week and I have no idea where that year went to. In fact, until talking to her mother the day before, the thought of her birthday quite slipped my mind. Of course, the child has no idea of what a birthday is, but her older sister has. So she is the one who would be cross with me if I forgot her sister's birthday. Anyway, I later asked Pádraig to get her something suitable — clothes or something — because I hate choosing presents when I have no idea what to get. That house is ridiculously full of toys.

Now, of course, I am saying that from a different perspective altogether. There were practically no toys when I was growing up. Or is it that I just can't remember that far back? Because my sons also say that they were very deprived when it came to toys. They cannot ever remember having much Meccanno or Lego or anything. But I know quite well that my sons had loads of stuff. I well remember the floor of the kitchen being strewn with their bits and pieces, and gathering it up into boxes and swearing that I'd hide half of it away and when I'd bring it out again, then they might have value on it.

But the mystery to me is, where did it all go? If it was still here, I'd have proof that my children did not have a deprived background. My second eldest son, Seamus, the one married in America, once said to me that we must have been very hard up when he was young because he remembered going to school with darned jumpers, and was that a fact?

Of course it was a fact. My mother always kept us supplied
with hand-knitted jumpers, and when she handed over the
new one she always gave me a full ball of wool as well for
the darning. My lively crowd were mighty hard on their
clothes and it never occurred to me to do anything else but
mend and make do. I am of the generation, after all, that
turned sheets side to middle when the middle wore thin. We
also cut up old towels for face cloths, and used all leftovers
for the next meal. Now, I never went as far as was done
when I was a child, cutting all the newspapers into squares
for use in the bathroom. That meant that there was no short-
age of reading material, even if at times it was frustrating to
have only half the story. Nowadays such a practice would
block all the drains and septic tanks. But sure we had none
of those either then. The house drains just joined up with the
nearest stream.

Now I must tell you a good one I heard during the week.
You know how a septic tank is supposed never to need
emptying if it is working properly — that all the waste gets
broken down and goes? Well, that rarely seems to happen
and many's the farmer who has to do a turn for the neighbours and empty their tanks with the slurry vacuum tank
and spread it on a field. And people think that the smell of
animal slurry is bad! In fact, some farmers I know, near
built-up areas, make money by allowing companies empty
the result of their clearing operations, on a regular basis,
into their slurry pits for later spreading. In Germany there is
a famous asparagus-growing area that is connected to the
town's waste disposal. Eoin was there once, on a farming
trip. Since it is asparagus season, however, I won't elaborate
any more on that subject.

But once again we forget. Night soil was once a most
valued product before the advent of artificial fertilisers. But
to get back to the septic tanks. The reason that they don't
work is the excessive cleanliness of the modern household
and the power of advertising. It is disinfectants for this, that

and the other thing — the loo, the floors, the counter tops, the sinks, the drains, and every scratch, cut and bruise a child gets. And why? Because that nice man on the ad says that otherwise you are not as nice/good/careful as you should be. And again, why is it always a man who tells the silly women in detergent advertisements how good the product is? That always annoys me.

Well, the net result of all those detergents and disinfectants is that the bacteria in the septic tank are killed off. But it seems you can have your cake and eat it — a bad metaphor that, for the subject matter in question. I was asked during the week, by a non-farmer, of course, if we ever had any small dead animals we wanted to dispose of. He would be ever so grateful if he could have it or them. He explained that he is dead and damned from trouble with his septic tank, but was advised that if he could get a dead dog or cat and throw it in, the natural bacteria would have a chance. His wife is excessively house proud.

Ever since, he is on the watch out for a dead rabbit, dog or cat on the road, and never can see one. I don't know where he is driving because I seem to see such things regularly. Anyway, we didn't have anything to oblige him with there and then. We do have a pit for dead calves, dug annually and covered in when the season is over; there is always the odd dead calf here. And frankly, in my opinion, the people who say to us that they never lose a calf must be condemned liars. But none of those dead calves were recent, and anyway it would be a bit big to transport. However, we did have something that he went off quite happily with, and that was a plastic bag full of cleanings.

I use the straw from the maternity pens for my garden, and if a cow does not eat her cleaning after calving, it is put into a plastic bag for disposal later, as it can become extremely smelly in hot weather. Now, how on earth did I start writing about my granddaughter's birthday and finish up with smelly afterbirths?

JUNE

A Garden Walk with a Difference

There is no doubt but that Liz Kavanagh must be the biggest fool in Ireland. That is precisely how I felt today, surrounded by my mugs of lemonade, with me feeling the biggest mug of all. You see, some weeks ago, this man I know — who not alone is a great gardener but also does tremendous work in that line for mentally handicapped youngsters — rang me up to ask if I would mind taking a group he was involved in, some Sunday in May.

I could hardly say no, could I, in the circumstances? I do have five fine boys, after all, and not a thing wrong with any of them, either mentally or physically. But I did wonder how safe my garden would be for a gang of thirty or so of his charges. Thirty, he told me would be the approximate number travelling.

'Good God, Liz, when will you ever learn to say no?' was Eoin's immediate reaction, as usual. As soon as he heard my full story, however, he said that of course he would be there to help. He is just as grateful as I am that all our children were born in perfect health. He is a pushover anyway for anything to help deprived children. So, the day before, he put in Trojan work removing all potential hazards like lawn mowers and clippers, and in making the rough ways smooth. Then, on the Sunday itself, he said he'd help me carry the refreshments out onto a table on the lawn.

We thought that would be better than having all the children in the house where there were too many breakables within reach. In the same way, I made great jugs of lemonade, ready to pour into mugs, lest the poor children could not cope with proper glasses. The eatables I planned in the same way for slow, awkward fingers. Eoin also had agreed that, if it was all right with them, he would take them on a bit of a farmyard tour to see some animals, especially the feeding of the last of the baby calves.

All done, we sat in the sun, reading the Sunday papers and awaiting the onslaught. 'I suppose they'll have a big bus,' said Eoin lazily as the appointed time approached. 'I do hope it will make it up the hill,' he added. 'Did you tell your friend to drop them all off at the entrance while the bus goes to park up in the yard?'

I, of course, had thought of no such thing. But it didn't matter anyway, because, next thing, we heard car after car coming up our hill and they all turned in the avenue. We were quickly on our feet then as Volvos, Mercedes and the like opened up to discharge some of the most affluently turned-out women this poor place has ever seen. Suffice it to say that if it was winter time their fur coats would have been tripping them. Instead, being a really hot day in early summer, their solid gold chains blinded us in the sunlight.

Eoin caught my eye over our mugs for lemonade and I could see that his jaw was dropping just as far as my own. Then I spotted my friend — the lone, soberly clad male among the bejewelled birds of paradise.

'What's this?' I gasped, dragging him aside with never a word of welcome. 'Who are all these women?'

'Why, Liz,' he replied, 'didn't I tell you about the group I have been giving a gardening course to [naming a very prestigious women's club in the city]? And I told them that they simply must come to see your place and all the work you do by yourself. Most of them haven't a clue actually, about real gardening....'

How he then laughed when I told him that I was expecting him to bring me a bus-load of retarded children. The gleam in his eye, however, warned me that he might yet have further trouble in store for me from that quarter.

In the meantime, I just did not know what to do. So, with no plausible story coming to mind, I decided that the truth it must be. No way could I hide my table full of mugs anyway. And, even more importantly, no way was I going to provide a proper afternoon tea for all that lot. I didn't have enough china cups for one thing, and anyway, my silver badly needed polishing.

So, I just welcomed them all and told them that they were the most over-privileged under-privileged children I had ever seen, and related the whole sorry saga. I then went on to remark that it helps to be somewhat mentally deficient anyway if one gets seriously into gardening. I have no doubt at all that gardening is a disease, and a progressive one at that.

Then, with all that off my chest, I invited them, not only to feel free to walk around and look at everything, but also to be children for the day and to sample my hospitality, such as it was. And do you know what, but it all went off marvellously. They — possibly because of their gardening course — were really interested in everything and some also knew enough to recognise the rarities of the plant world when they were pointed out to them.

Though I must admit of recent years I have been somewhat wary of pointing out my very special pets to people, ever since I once took a certain woman I was trying to impress, for a tour of my garden. I kept on pointing out all my rare and exotic specimens, little realising I was rapidly losing my audience of one. But soon I was left in no doubt on this matter when she, pointing out some plain self-seeded marigolds, said, with a peculiar inflexion in her voice, 'And I suppose those are something very special, rare and unusual too?'

Then, for once in my life, the perfect answer popped out of my head at this put down. Normally I think of the perfect rejoinder only hours later when it is miles too late. This time, however, without thinking, I was speaking the truth, with no malice aforethought, when I replied, 'I suppose you could say that, in a way. They are special all right. I like these marigolds because these are the Flowers of Hope, the seeds of which were given out a couple of years ago for every subscription made to the Remedial Clinic.

'This year it was sunflower seeds and I planted them out over there,' I continued, all innocent, as I pointed to where those sunflowers stood so proudly high in another border. My visitor had the grace to blush.

My group, today, especially their leader, were amused at that story, which I told when we came across yet more self-sown descendants of those original seeds. It was that self-same clinic I thought was coming to visit my garden today. Anyway, after their walk around and all my talking, my ladies drank their lemonade, out of the mugs, and ate their bread and jam and ice cream in wafers. They seemed to enjoy it too, as they sat about the place in the sun. Then one of them said, 'Now, Eoin, what about that trip around the farm you promised? Can't we see that too? I'd just love to feed baby calves. And I promise that we'll be very, very good!'

I didn't altogether like the sound of that, especially when the last I saw of Eoin was him disappearing up to the yard, surrounded by beauteous females. And I would swear that the blonde swinging off his arm had an all over-tan, from the glimpse I got of the heavy, gold chain disappearing suggestively down her décolletage. Ah well. It all started out as being in a good cause. And that young blonde won't get far up the farmyard anyway with those strappy high-heeled sandals of hers. She won't get far with Eoin either if my judgement is right. She just isn't his type!

Flown from the Coop

We were at a silver wedding party this week of a cousin of
mine — a really big affair. It was a very mixed age group
with much more strangers than relations present. Actually, I
strongly suspect that the party was as much a business affair
as a celebration. There weren't many farmers there and
that's for sure.

I can't talk about golf since I am not a golfer. The only
other subject of interest for most of the women was cooking
or their children, while the men went on and on about sport,
especially their golf, rugby and sailing. So, wherever possible, I chose the lesser of the evils, the talk about children.
And Eoin also seemed to gravitate towards the groups of
women.

I think that, as a result of some of the family histories we
heard, we both came home from there decidedly glad that
our children are not really young any more, and that we
survived the worst and lived to tell the tale. We are facing
into our pearl anniversary this autumn — thirty years married — so are that one step ahead, in the ages of our children, than those boasting lesser anniversaries.

However, I'll tell you this much first: we didn't celebrate
the occasion of our own silver wedding anniversary in
proper style at all! We had a few friends to the house to
celebrate with us. And, while we did them well, that was it.
The silver wedding bashes we have been at lately, however,
have all started with a full Church ceremony. They com-
menced with the couple formally walking up the aisle. Then
there was a formal renewal of vows, followed by a special
Mass, with, in the congregation, many of those who were at
the original wedding ceremony, as well as the family and
friends acquired since.

For the first such celebration we got a silver-edged invi-
tation, stating when, where, and how (black tie no less). I

thought the whole church thing a bit much. But, do you know, in actual fact, I found that ceremony extremely touching. It must be the incurable romantic in me. It was great to see a middle-aged man, take the hand of his wife of twenty-five years and publicly pledge his love for her all over again. It was done with obvious love between the pair of them, surrounded as they were by their children, now well on their way to being full-grown men and women.

The husband did the reading at the Mass, and, as he read about a good woman being a pearl beyond price, he smiled at his wife, that private little smile all of us long-married couples develop. It would do your heart great good to see that smile. I noticed a lot of other long-married couples also turning and smiling at one another, and it was all so touching because isn't there great comfort in that special smile of private understanding?

I only wish some of my own young people I hear regularly mouthing off about there being no point in marriage nowadays could be at a few of these silver wedding do's. Then, they'd see that things do last, and get better and better with the years. I'd say the exact same to any young couple struggling with marital problems right now. We all went through that stage too, though we might not care to admit it now. There are stages when you wonder why you ever got married, as love ebbs and flows. But, take it from one who knows, as surely as the tide of love goes out and all seems dry and arid, that warm feeling of love also returns. So, remembering this helps, because, just as surely it will leave again for yet another period, so it will return, just as the real tide also ebbs and flows.

The longer I live, the more I am convinced that no family is really unique. We all seem to go through all the same stages of life, no matter how remarkable we may privately think we are. Parents of young children are convinced that they have somehow bred little geniuses and that their little darlings will never give them any trouble. I have even heard parents of pre-teen children say that properly brought-up children just don't give trouble, and this said with the greatest self-righteousness: God help their innocent and ignorant heads.

And then, parents of teenaged children at their very worst become convinced that they will never survive it. It appears to them that there was never a child as impossible and terrible as their own tormentor. At that party I heard a lot about teenage problems, possibly because it is known that we have been through the mill ourselves and emerged reasonably sane and relatively good friends with all our children.

As far as I can gather, no family runs smoothly at this teenage stage, no matter how good a public face they may put on things. And this need to pretend that all is perfect puts additional strain on parents at what is a bad time anyway. If they would only let others know what is happening, they would not feel so terribly alone. Trouble with teenagers is not always a reflection on the parents, except in the eyes of those not yet at that stage. Time will cook their goose for them too!

Nobody can begin to imagine the suffering of this time until they have personal experience of it all. Up to this, you just do not have a notion of the pain parents suffer, since your own teenaged memories colour your personal feelings. Then, it was so easy to blame your parents for family troubles, and you determine to do so very much better when your turn comes, fully convinced it is possible. But the shoe does pinch very badly when you are the one who is wearing it.

That night I was desperately sorry for the mother of a seventeen-year-old son — her eldest — who is really going off the rails. She could talk to me about it, she said, because didn't we have a lot of trouble with one of our sons too when he was seventeen? The submerged pain rushed back to invade my heart once again as she spoke.

That particular son — our pride and joy, our farmer-to-be ever since he was just a tiny lad — had left home one morning, with nothing but a note left on the breakfast table for us, saying he was gone for good and that we would never see him again. He was exactly seventeen years and seven weeks old at the time my nice complacent world came crashing about my ears.

'I can't talk to anyone,' my new acquaintance confided. 'Nobody else has the troubles we seem to have and I have no idea where I went so wrong.'

God love her. I well remember feeling just as terribly isolated and alone when our sons started creating in their teens. All the other children I knew appeared to be angelic in comparison to mine, who were turning into daylight demons. Our children appeared both to despise and, indeed, actively to hate us, their parents. Peace departed from this house for years, the very public running away by one son being but the final straw.

This had been preceded by endless battles about school work not being done, their clothes, their hairstyles, their music, their friends. There was hardly a door left intact in the house with the ferocious banging they all got from time to time. Sons point blank refused to go to Mass. They answered back for no good reason at all. Their bedrooms were like pig-sties. Honestly, the list was endless and only got worse when they started going out late at night, and taking the car or the jeep, when we were gone to bed and they were not all of age, or insured, to drive same. Then there were the accidents ... I really do not want to remember the details.

Those were bad years, make no mistake about it. We worried day and night. But, for us, there was also the very real pain of the loss of the child who totally cut himself off. Yet we all suffer the pain of the loss of our children, to a greater or lesser extent, as they struggle into full adulthood and finally leave home. We lose our dreams for them as they live their own dreams, of which we are not a part.

Of course, now, with the benefit of hindsight, I can see that our pride was part of the problem. I recall suffering badly those years when the exam results came out and friends rang up to know how mine had done, when they really couldn't care less. All they wanted was to boast about their own children. I never had results I could boast about. And yet what difference did that make in the long run? My sons all seem to have fitted in all right and made reasonable adults, despite all their terrible teens. But that was as much in spite of me, perhaps, as because of me. I was not happy being brought back to the memories of those bad times, by this woman who had button-holed me at this party.

'I would do things differently,' I finally admitted to her ... and to myself. But that is easy enough to say with the twenty-twenty vision of hindsight. At the time we did what we thought was best was for each and every one of our sons.

But, again with hindsight, I think that my pride in my children was an extension of myself. I wanted them to conform to what I thought was best. So now I say, what do hairstyles or clothes matter? They each only rebelled for a few short years and I learned to roll with the punches as time went on and I grew to expect less from each son in turn, and they were all the better for it. I should also have rolled with the punches with the older ones.

I said all this to the poor suffering mother. But I doubt very much if I did her any good. Her pain is very much her own private property still, as she nurses it carefully. She is still at the stage of waking up in the middle of the night, crying for what might have been. She has yet to accept that what she really is mourning is the loss of her own dreams for her dearly loved eldest child.

Only time really helps with the loss of anything, even one's hopes for one's children. If there is any cure for family disappointments, I, for one, never found it. And each family has at least one member who gives them serious cause for heartache. But you do forget it all with time, and the majority of lost sheep do make contact again, even if they never really return to the fold.

All Kinds of Exams to be Faced

This week I am not at all well, and it is no earthly use anybody telling me that I brought it all on myself. I know I did.
It just seemed like a good idea at the time, going back to
college and getting a degree, and now here I am, four years
later, and I wonder if I am any the wiser. My final exams
start tomorrow and I am climbing the walls. I'm not eating
or sleeping properly. I snap if anybody so much looks at me,
and all because I am filled with blind terror at what those
papers will show when I start to read down the exam paper
tomorrow morning at half past nine. Will the questions I
have so painstakingly prepared be the ones that come up?
Will I look at it and recognise nothing at all? Will my memory fail me entirely? Dare I sneak in a few prompts written
on the palm of my hand? Should I write down all the key
points before ever the exam papers are given out, so that I
do not forget them?

Honestly, I am a nervous wreck and it really does not
matter a damn, except to my pride, whether I do well or
even fail. There are some that might even like me to fail. I
was once told I only went to college for a 'besting match'
anyway! Could you beat that? That comment really knocked
the wind out of my sails and I was only telling my story of
my very first assessment in First Arts.

Our papers were given back to us before the lecture that
night. So, of course, we all sneaked a quick look at our
marks, and where possible those of our neighbours. We
could only know how good or bad we were by comparing
ourselves with others. I was personally over the moon with
mine, that one time. Then, at our break, one young man
leant across to me and said, in all seriousness. 'I hate to God
to be beaten by a woman, Liz! But to be beaten by a woman
of your age f---s me up entirely.'

I was surprised, but not because of the use of the F word.

God knows I've heard that often enough in the mouths of the young in college, both male and female. No, I was shocked more by the blatant display of both sexism and ageism from such a young man. My immediate response was to say to myself, 'You ain't seen anything yet, buster....' His reaction was part of the reason I didn't give up any-where along the line. He did, however, after the diploma. I was too stubborn to give in, and now look where that has got me.

I can tell you this much though. I am now full of sympa-thy for anybody doing their Leaving or Junior Cert next week. But it will be all right once you sit down and get started. It is the uncertainty that is the killer. At least that is the way it has been for me these past four years, so why should my finals be any different? I have put in the work and nobody ever knows everything.

There is a much greater uncertainty hanging over us here anyway, and that's why the family haven't a great deal of sympathy for me and my own personal troubles.

Last week the Department was on to our vet, who was on to us, to have our next herd test as soon as possible, and Monday was the day fixed. That means tomorrow is the reading of the test when we will know our fate this time. In our last test, six weeks ago, twenty-one cows went down, which was a crushing blow. The bulk tank was where it affected us worst, which will be echoed, of course, in our next milk cheque. Once the cows were gone, they were gone.

Now here it all is again, facing us once more, and we have no idea what the outcome will be. We may go clear or we may be facing into another big loss. It isn't like doing an exam, where, if you have the work done, you are reasonably confident, whatever about the pre-exam nerves. But what can you do about TB, except pray?

The Department was out about badgers a month or so ago and a piece of waste ground was bulldozed between two neighbouring farms, who are also locked up even longer than us. Now, I believe — and I have only what I hear — that there were badgers flying left, right and centre when the bulldozer cut through their setts. One of them even had a whole load of fodder beet drawn up to the opening of that sett.

That I do know to be true, because the man who saw it told me about it himself. He also said that there is no bother knowing an active sett because of all the fresh activity around it. Now, God knows, we have looked for setts all over the place here in recent times and never found anything. We hear all sorts of things you can do if you do happen to find an active sett but the opportunity for us to try any of them did not arise.

One was to soak sausages in paraquat, or stuff them with rat bait, and leave them near the sett. Not that anybody I know did anything like that, of course! The Department, instead, has been out there officially trapping badgers. They are rumoured to have caught seven and four of them tested positive for TB. So you can gather that the badger is being blamed for all our misfortunes.

And a test is a misfortune and a herd test is always bad for the very simple reason that everybody is clear only until their next test. So I hate a herd test at the best of times. It is worst, however, at this time of the year, just when the cows are at last milking well. A herd test always upsets the cows, all that pushing them through the cattle race, injecting them and taking their numbers. A set-back now means they are back for the rest of the year.

It is only just now that grass is really growing well here. All spring we have been chasing every blade of grass as it grew. There was no need for topping and that's for sure, since the cows skinned each paddock that little bit too bare at each grazing. Funny expression to use, skinning a field, but that is just what they were doing. It was like taking the fur off a rabbit.

Long ago that used to be done, and the rabbit skin then

cured in the smoke over the fire. When cured, they used to
make the loveliest of in-soles for all our boots and wellingtons. Once it came to summer then, all would be discarded
and we could run barefoot and feel the mud squelch deli-
ciously up between our toes on a hot day. My daughters-in-
law are shocked at the thought of that — everybody has got
so squeaky clean these days. But certain things marked
certain seasons and we all knew where we were.

There was no trouble in those days with herd tests and
that's for sure. But actually it wasn't as much trouble on
Monday as we feared because the vet came grand and early
and there was no blood. What shorthand we use in everyday life. I said that to one of my college friends talking
about why I wasn't free that morning to go to her house, to
go over our course before the exams, and she immediately
thought, when I said 'no blood', that animals were normally
bleeding all over the place. She got quite uptight about the
cruelty of it all.

Ah well, she and I will be sitting our first exam tomorrow
when the cows will I hope be passing theirs. So, by tomorrow night, I will know the worst.

The Bishop's Boy

Michaella, when I asked her how school was, told me that
they were out practising their clapping every day and the
big children were out practising their singing.

'And Diyee I am not to talk to you or Dad-Dad when you
come to my school on Monday. I am to stand in a straight
line and clap mad, and the whole place is all cleaned up.'

The sweet innocence of the child, I thought, and her calm
assurance that we too would be at the grand official opening
of an extension to our local national school. Children at that
age are so certain that the world revolves around them. So,

of course, we went. Anyway, her daddy, my son, is now treasurer of the local parents' group which helps to fund the school. So we also went to support him.

Now, he is not on the management committee, which is another thing again. His lot's main function in life is to ensure sufficient funds are in place, not only to pay the figure per child required for the official running of the place, but also to provide much-needed extras. Pádraig just went to a parents' meeting last year and came home with the job of treasurer. Then, and only then, was I impressed to learn that our local lotto, run by the athletics club, is divided equally between that club and the schools of the parish. I was even more impressed when I discovered from my son quite how much it makes each week.

I am a firm believer that your chances of winning the national lottery are only marginally improved by buying a ticket. So I'm afraid that attitude of mine extended to this lottery as well. But I did regularly recognise the names of the people who won. So, most of the parish, evidently, were great supporters of it. Now, I know that this is because it is really a painless extraction of funds for the school. Because of my grandchildren I too now have the weekly flutter.

I know, from when I was a parent with children at that school, what it is like trying to collect money. Eoin was the very first 'Bishop's boy' chosen by the then parish priest to serve as one of his representatives on the management committee. It was such a new thing then to let the parents have any say in the running of the school. But of course it soon transpired that the committee's main, and indeed only, function in life, was to raise money. And I often stood with Eoin outside the church gate doing precisely that. There were no such things as lotteries in those days unfortunately.

People, however, were extremely generous. Nobody really passed us by. Even a long-term bachelor gave me a pound note one Sunday, when a pound was a lot of money, He said that he'd never know the day he might need a school for his own children! That brought a great laugh from all the men standing around at the church gate — which was precisely what he had intended of course. I did not enjoy standing at the church gate, for not a lot of money.

So it was an education to me this week to see all that has now been bought by the local lotto funds. That open day I would have loved to have seen their computer, and its programmes, in action. The lotto also pays for swimming lessons, with the children bussed to the nearest pool. There are speech and drama classes, a fridge for the children's lunches, a bus shelter so that they don't have to stand in the rain waiting for the school bus to come, and so on. In fact, I suspect they will shortly be in danger of running out of ideas for extra spending.

But the regular spending will always be there. They even give the children parties from time to time — Sports-day, Christmas and Halloween and the like. And when I say parties I do mean parties. It is not a question of two sweets per child and calling it a party.

It was a really nostalgic morning for me, talking to those I personally went to school with, or those who had children going there the same time as ours. 'Do you remember?' peppered every conversation. I was reminded, more than once, how the making of Eoin into the 'Bishop's boy' did not work out perhaps quite as had been intended. Eoin was so disappointed at the time to find that our then parish priest seemed to think he owned the school. He never could come to terms with the fact that the parents could have any power in any department at all. His whole attitude of 'I have decided' drove Eoin, for one, absolutely bananas. Eoin never was a yes man.

The school was then a two-teacher, one-room school, with dividing doors, and was quite overcrowded. The parents, with the zeal of a brand-new committee, went to endless trouble to get permission for a third teacher and a new room. That extension, twenty-five years ago now, was a prefab, and the third teacher months away. The numbers of pupils had to hit a certain level for so many months before an extra teacher actually arrived

With the prefab ready and furnished, it made sense to move one of the teachers out there and give the master and his pupils proper room and quietness. There were four to each two-child desk at this stage, and every sound carried quite clearly through the folding door. The then parish priest, however, refused to hand over the key. Week after week went by and he was quite impervious to questions and deputations. Feelings started to run high in the parish.

Finally, one Saturday morning, Eoin and another parent from the management committee went to the school, broke the lock on the prefab and moved in all that was needed from the main building. Then they opened up the dividing doors and left all ready for Monday morning. Both men went there again, early on the Monday morning, to ensure that things stayed changed — which they did and there was not even a whisper about it, ever, from the parochial house.

But, perhaps not surprisingly, Eoin was not re-appointed when his term in office was up.

JULY

Korky Kavanagh

'No way!' has been my reaction each and every time my sons have wanted to get a new dog. And poorly enough they took this as recently as yesterday. I know we are one dog down since poor Sally just disappeared, and our red setter is pretty senile by now.

'She's no fun any more' said our youngest. 'She won't run and play — just goes moping about....' Ah, the exuberance of youth!

Eoin Óg still runs from A to B for the sheer pleasure of it, while I, like my old dog, proceed with measured tread. 'A pup would be great for playing with next winter in the snow,' he went on, warming to his theme and this on a hot day in July.

I fervently hoped we'd get neither pup nor snow either now or next winter. Either would mean sheer pleasure to him at any time but I know, from bitter experience, the added work that both cause, not to mind the danger. I mean, would you take on a full-grown pure-bred black Rottweiler? That's what they wanted to do a few weeks ago. A friend of theirs was willing to give it to them — 'for nothing', they added, pointing out that normally such dogs, with papers, cost hundreds of pounds. Life hasn't yet taught them that that people rarely give away anything that is of real value. There must be a jolly good reason why they are looking for a good home in the country for their dog.

It wasn't the first time by any means that we have heard the excuse of town houses being too small for dogs. We have been offered several Alsations over the years. Once we were even asked to take on a Great Dane. Quite honestly, however, I am half afraid of those watchdog breeds. They can be quite vicious if they are not handled properly. It is all very well to say that we need a guard dog on the place. but who, I ask, is to guard us against the guard-dog? And anyway they are much too big and no way do I want any dog in the house any more, not to mind a great big one.

I remember only too well the damage done over the years when my sons were young, to my house, garden, or even the washing on the line. Young boys and dogs are an inevitable combination, especially in the countryside. My sons used to lavish on their dogs all the affection they seemed unable to give to their parents. Wouldn't you think that by now, with fiancées and the giving away of girl-friends, they'd no longer have that need?

Korky is the dog of theirs I most remember, for many reasons. When I'd go to call them in the mornings, for school, he would always be found in under the bedclothes with one of them. He also went to school with them most days. In those days, children either walked or cycled to school and were not driven everywhere as seems to happen today. So it is no longer possible, I suppose, for a dog to delight a classroom of youngsters as our Korky did once.

He spent most days either in the playground or under one of their school desks. He was under the desk the day when the Master raised his stick to one of my offspring. Probably this was with due cause, I may add, knowing that particular son only too well. But, before the stick landed on the outstretched palm, Korky growled and, with threatening lip, sprang straight upwards at the teacher. Fortunately, for everybody, the man's heavy tweed jacket (no central heating twenty years ago) saved bloodshed. And the teacher had a sense of humour as well. Both child and dog were spared

retribution. It was safer for him, the Master said to me ruefully later. Yet Korky continued to escort them to school on
and off, whenever he escaped my watchful eye. The likes of
that wouldn't happen today. But then again, there is no
corporal punishment either these days in schools, whatever
about the home.

Korky wasn't having a hand laid on any of the boys, at
home or abroad, and I still have the marks to prove it. One
famous wet Saturday, I came into the house to find five pairs
of wellington boots scattered to the four corners of the back
kitchen. The place was strewn with bits of bread and jam,
and the noise of my sons, playing cards, was deafening. I
was tired and somewhat edgy — the time of the month no
doubt. Then, just as I came to remonstrate with my sons,
John, in a pure fit of temper, caught the table and over-
turned it: cards, cups, the lot. I was pretty mad as I made for
him — then he was still smaller than I. Just as I started to
shake him thoroughly, however, Korky sprang.

I don't know whether it was the scared look on John's
face or the half-strangled cry he gave when I grabbed him
that made Korky spring to his defence. But leap he did and
sank his teeth into the most available portion of my anatomy — my bottom. Then, before I knew it, there was a mass
exodus out the back door, with Korky safely tucked under
Seamus's arm. Letting go my grip of John, to inspect the
damage to my rear end, next thing I knew he had scuttled
out the back door as well.

There I was, left standing all alone in the field of battle,
with the blood just starting to trickle. I could still hear the
strangled laughter of my sons as they disappeared to safety
up the yard. I myself wasn't sure whether I'd best laugh or
cry. Eoin was in a similar pickle when he came rushing in a
few moments later. The boys, in their flight, told him that
he'd better get in to Mom fast. But I can tell you this much.
It was just as well for Eoin that he chose not to laugh — well
not right then anyway.

Korky Kavanagh, as he was known to all the school-children, died of extreme old age in the end, deeply mourned by all, even myself. Several other dogs, however, met untimely ends with us over the years. Farmyards are the most dangerous places for dogs despite what our city friends appear to think. A freshly calved cow, in defence of her calf no doubt, once did for a lovely collie of ours. Shep had gone into the calving pen in search of a nice fresh after-birth, and the cow battered him to death for his greed. Then there was the dog who ate rat bait and died despite several trips to the vet and I don't know how many blood transfu-sions. More than one met his fate under tractor wheels, and another got a horrible death in the baler. It had the bad habit of running in circles around the tractor and described too short a circle its final time.

But the most dangerous place of the lot is the slurry pits. Any pup or dog who goes into one of those hasn't a hope. They are wired up against cattle all right. But dogs in full chase can get anywhere. One major tragedy occurred when a heap of dung was left, temporarily, against the seven-foot-high wall of the pit. The boys had two pups that year — the unplanned offspring of our redsetter bitch who, because of their coaxing, hadn't gone for sailors like the rest of the siblings. Beautiful little things they turned out to be, half neighbouring Labrador, and spoilt by us all. Anyway, one morning, they were both missing. After a long day of tears and heartbreaking searching, Eoin found the poor bedrag-gled corpses floating in the slurry. They had climbed up to the top of the heap of dung, obviously, and so into the pit. How can any parent console a child for the loss of a much loved pet? Our only consolation ourselves was that it was a very salutary warning to us for the future. Anywhere a puppy can go, so too may a small child.

So, we were well warned of the hideous dangers of slurry pits long before grandchildren could come. Our own chil-dren were well to the age of reason before we built our first slurry pit. Protection, therefore, against cattle was all we bothered with, and that not always successfully if gates were left open! But that is another story and it's dogs, with good cause, that are on my mind this week. Yesterday, when getting up, I heard all this yelping coming from the room of Pádraig, our engaged son.

When I went to investigate I found the loveliest little golden Labrador there in a box, all cosy on one of Pádraig's good jumpers, but lonely of course. Then, before Pádraig was in from the cows for his breakfast, I had Sara, my daughter-in-law-to-be, on the phone to me, looking for him, of course, but rhapsodising in the meantime about the pup, her present from him. She thought it was such a good idea to have her dog used to the place it would be living in. Under the sheer force of her enthusiasm I knew I was lost. A dog in the house I knew I was going to have, despite all my protestations to the contrary only the day before. And the new arrival helped me to dress the beds, once I had lifted it up the stairs. I just couldn't leave it all lonesome down there looking up at me, now could I? A little early training I'm having against the day the grandchildren come, is what Eoin says is happening, as he steadfastly refuses to have anything at all to do with the little dote. I do hope he will change his tune before a grandchild arrives.

Oh Mother!

Wasn't there once a song or was it a poem, about 'mother' being the loveliest word in the English language? Well, if you were living around here for a while you'd soon forget that romantic notion. Then you'd know the scorn that can be expressed in just two simple words. 'Oh Mother!' is something I frequently hear. It has even come to the stage where I now term 'mother' as nothing less than a term of abuse!

All I have to do to bring an impatient 'Oh Mother!' down on top of my innocent head may be only to suggest that those sons of mine do something in a different way, or indeed ask if something has been done yet. This intolerant 'Oh Mother!' is always accompanied by a despairing casting of the eyes up to heaven. My opinions on any subject under the sun, be it from farming to their friends or their behaviour, elicit a further 'Oh Mother!', and such deep despairing sighs that I am rapidly thinking of going on permanent retreat — to the silence of a retreat anyway, whatever about the prayers.

And you know it is no time since I used to be plain Mom to them all the time, ever since they put aside the Mammy of their national school days. Now I am only Mom to them the rare occasions they are being fond of me, or the frequent occasions they want something from me! Ah well! It is just another, and hopefully the last, stage in their development. They want to prove that, not alone do they not need me now, but they can't, for the life of them, understand why they ever did depend on me. This could upset me greatly, if I didn't gather from various friends and acquaintances, that my lot are no worse than most, and indeed are better than many.

Our conversations on this topic have led some of us beleaguered mothers to think that there could be a great opening for setting up a society for the protection of parents from adult children. Talking to each other about our offspring has proved to us that we are now all suffering somewhat similar fates.

'Such a feed of abuse, I had to put up with from Jack a few nights ago!' said one woman to me, as she opened up on her problems. 'The things that boy said to me, no mother should ever hear from her child....'

'It's the whispering together they do about me, that drives me mad — with the whispers always just loud enough for me to hear, ' interrupted another. 'And just about everything has to be my fault,' she continued. 'Everything I ever did wrong, when they were small, is now thrown in my face.... The final straw for me was when Mary came home, after a fight with her husband, and she said that I had marked her for life, and all because I wouldn't let her have a light on in her bedroom when she was small.... I ask you.... Could any one at all make sense of that? And I wouldn't mind but I have no recollection whatsoever of her ever having been afraid of the dark. But I had to sit there and take it, because the more I tried to justify myself, the more the rest of the family joined forces with her, against me, and the more wicked they all became with their memories.'

She was nearly in tears again with the memory of it as, enthralled, we asked whether Mary had gone back to her husband. Fights with a husband and night lights — that admixture led to all sorts of combinations in our fertile imaginations. But Mary had gone back to her husband that very night, after the catharsis of the attack by herself and her siblings on her poor mother. She — the mother — then went on to tell us how her daughter was on the phone the very next morning, as though nothing at all had happened the night before.

'And then she accused me of sulking, when, naturally enough, I was somewhat silent and distant with her. It nearly started another row,' she concluded sadly.

I know we were only getting one side of the story. However, since each one of us had suffered something similar, it rang uncomfortably true in our ears, especially that bit about children saying the most dreadful things to their parents, and then expecting their parents to be exactly the same to them as always. Parents, it seems, are to remember nothing, feel no pain and hold no grudges, while their children remember, and nourish, every hurt and harm done to them since birth.

So, there and then, the group of us set about drawing up a set of rules for a Society for the Support of Parents of Adult Children. We were to be the five founder members, and actually we had no difficulty at all in laying out our rules.

- Rule one: Whatever we do, or have done, in the upbringing of our children is probably wrong, but this does not now matter in the slightest. Anything else would have been equally wrong. And, besides, we only did the best we could with the material we had. Therefore, self doubts and/or any accusations by adult children are completely out of order.

- Rule two: One parent must never side with adult children against the other parent. Adult children are all adept in their use of the 'divide and conquer' precept. Allowing this to happen is foolish in the extreme and extremely hurtful to the other partner. Remember that the injured spouse will still be there that night, and remembering, when the child in question has already forgotten and is gone about his or her own life again.

- Rule three: No adult child must ever be allowed to interfere in any way with the personal life of his or her parents.

However, to implement rule three you may first have to repossess your home! Children have a way of progressively and irritatingly claiming everything in your house as theirs. They start in the pram, with the attention of all visitors to the house. Then they go on to monopolise the radio, the TV, the car, the living room, especially when they have friends in, and even the kitchen whenever they, or the said friends, feel hungry.

Nothing of yours is sacred from their depredations. Your very best notepaper, your shampoo or carefully hoarded bath-salts, every pen or nail scissors you ever bought — these just disappear, as do socks, tights, and, above all, handkerchiefs.

You must not even look at anything in their bedrooms while they cheerfully rifle through every drawer in yours. You have to give up buying in stocks of many items, from biscuits to beer, which you once kept for the unexpected guests. And how often do you find your family using every appliance in the place, from the bath to the screwdriver, and above all the phone, at precisely the moment you yourself need them?

We gave up at this stage because the list could go on and on. What we all really needed were ideas on how to go about this repossession of hearth and home. And perhaps we also need more rules for our list. I could start by asking my family for suggestions. But I know all I'd hear would be 'Oh Mother!' with even deeper sighs than usual.

Patrimony, Parsimony, Matrimony, Alimony

The young pair were off doing their pre-marriage course last weekend, as is required by our church before they get married. Now I know that rarely do young couples have a good word to say about these courses, considering them a quite unnecessary imposition. My pair, however, came home on the Sunday night full of the joys of life, having enjoyed themselves thoroughly for the day — though I am not at all sure that enjoyment was the object of the exercise in the eyes of the organisers.

I, of course, asked them what it was about, and they both burst into laughter, looked at each other, and then Eoin Óg answered, 'Sex and money, Mom — what else?'

'Well at least you learned enough to couple the two.' I retorted, but I was secretly very pleased that they were happy about the whole thing. I was really expecting them to have religion shoved down their throats all day, and that, I knew, would have raised their hackles in no uncertain manner, and a discussion on anything to do with the merits or demerits of religion with Eoin in the room is usually best avoided.

'There was a lot about mothers-in-law too,' Lisa then added.

'Oh?' I said, not quite sure what would come next because you can never be sure how young people really feel deep down, beneath all the lip service.

'Well,' she replied, 'mothers-in-law seemed to be an awful worry to most of the girls there, but I said to them that my mother-in-law had once written an article, many years ago, which I photocopied and kept....'

'Oh?' I said, again interrupting, fearing the worst because regularly things I have written about come back to haunt me, or are even used as evidence against me if and when it suits. I had no recollection of ever writing much about mothers-in-law before I got to that stage myself.

'How did you come by that if it was so long ago?' I asked.

'It was when I was in college and first started going out with Eoin Óg,' explained Lisa. 'They always have the current copies of the *Farmers' Journal* there, and I was able to order all the back issues from the archives. So, I had a great time reading back about all the things they used to do when they were young — at school, their first girlfriends and all that — and I photocopied a lot of the ones I particularly wanted.'

'But I didn't even know you then, Lisa,' I quickly intervened, in self-defence against whatever was coming.

She, however, put me out of my misery, while giving me grounds for thought as well. She said that even when they were still all at school I was constantly making comments about how it all depended on the girl they married and things like that.

I think she's wrong about that being a preoccupation of mine, but she's the one who went to the trouble of looking up the back issues. She has promised to bring me out her photocopies, which I would love to see, not to remind me of what I wrote all those years ago, because I now fear they would embarrass me hugely, but to find out what she, my future daughter-in-law, regarded as significant.

Then, over my kitchen table, she asked me straight out who I was writing about when I said that, for one woman I knew, if the Blessed Virgin herself came down on earth again, she wouldn't be good enough for that woman's only son! Then the old memory banks began to work again all right. But of course no way was I going to satisfy their curiosity. Too much Lisa may have found out about me already from the archives.

She said, however, that what I had written, and she had photocopied, was that a mother's love is different; that there is no competition for the love of the husband/son; that neither really takes from the other if both sides only exercise a little plain, ordinary common sense; that just as a father loves a daughter, and his wife, dearly, at the same time, but in quite different ways, so can a son love his mother and his wife too, at the one and the same time, and one does not take from the other.

Indeed, if I were writing that article again, I could add that affectionate sons tend to make good husbands because they are in the habit of loving. I wonder if a lot of those girls who dislike their mothers-in-law are really jealous, and fearful that their man has not enough love for both wife and mother. They should remember that he is their 'man', but a son only to the mother-in-law. There is no contest really.

'So, what else did you do at your course?' I asked, getting them back on track. It appears that they filled out several questionnaires about each other — about all sorts of things from favourite foods to colours, what each was earning, what each thought it would cost to run a house for a week, priorities in life, number of children wanted, all sorts of things like that. Now, there was no judging of their answers, no points system as to whether or not they were a suitable match. Each just got a copy of their partner's questionnaire to compare with their own perceptions of themselves, and no doubt to draw their own conclusions.

Anyway, apropos that, they said that there was no justification for the remark made to them when they were booking this course originally. Then they were told, quite bluntly, that they were leaving it too late entirely. And when they asked why, they were told, in all seriousness, that there was always the fear that they might find out something there, at the course, that would cause them to change their minds. So obviously there were no shocks in their questionnaire answers.

'What about the sex talk?' I next queried, being full of curiosity as to precisely how much was covered.

But the answer I got was a slightly embarrassed, 'You know yourself, Mom!' and I suppose if I don't by now it is a bad look out. Anyway, they were told nothing that they didn't know already I discovered, even though they had a doctor there for the full afternoon, on that job.

The one thing they did discover that surprised them were all the reasons the Church has for annulments. Most of those I already knew, but there was one new one on me. Presuming that my pair have got it right, the Church will now consider as grounds for annulment any pre-marriage understanding a couple makes, be it verbal or written, to divorce if things don't work out.

That I found quite extraordinary, especially with a divorce referendum pending here. I have already heard some engaged young people saying jokingly, in my hearing, that if it didn't work out they could always divorce, because divorce will definitely be legalised in the referendum. But does that mean that even half-joking like that, in front of witnesses, would give them grounds for an annulment in the eyes of the Catholic Church if things were to go wrong? That sounds daft to me. But if it is true, perhaps they should indeed play safe and put such thoughts in writing beforehand just in case they want to have their cake and eat it too? The whole thing makes me feel decidedly nervous. Just as well it wasn't a son of mine that was being so flippant that day, in front of witnesses, about the possibility of divorce.

But all this talk, with our heir apparent and his future

wife, did make me remember another article I wrote some time ago about the impossibility of young people getting into farming in Ireland, with quotas for this, that, and the other thing. I then used the old saying about there being traditionally only three ways, in Ireland, to acquire a farm of land.

These are patrimony, parsimony and matrimony — you inherit it from your father; live miserably while you save up for it; or else find yourself somebody with a nice farm, and marry them. But the thought occurred to me there, at my kitchen table, that shortly there may well be a fourth way as well to acquire your farm of land. What if it becomes a case of patrimony, parsimony, matrimony and alimony? There's a thought for you to follow on those thoughts on Church annulments!

Disease in the Area

The main talking point around here, this week, is that a near neighbour has suffered a brucellosis breakdown. So we are all in a state of panic. Weird and wonderful are the stories going the rounds about how the brucellosis infection came into the area, but as Eoin said to the lads, that is not the important point. The important thing is to contain it now that it is here.

But how to do that is the worry. Ours is a completely self-contained herd. We only buy in stock bulls. Our bounds fences are secure. We never had a break-in between ourselves and this particular neighbour. But wildlife is no respecter of fences. If an animal aborts in a neighbouring field, foxes, grey-jackets, crows, anything, can bring the infected bits and pieces into us. So, I am not exaggerating when I say we are running scared.

The very first thing we did when we got the news from

the Department of Agriculture was to phone up our co-op to find out when was the last ring test for brucellosis and how we did in it. It was something of a relief to find that we were clear anyway the week after the infected animal calved down next door to us. And there is to be another routine ring test next week. So another phone call will let us know the result of that. But, as was explained to us, the co-op is legally obliged to inform the Department of any positive result in a ring test, so we would hear fast from that source if we were in trouble.

I must give praise where it is due and tell you that a man from the Department was the first to break the news to us, over the phone, before the notice ever came in the post. He explained, exactly and painstakingly, precisely what had happened and what it would mean for us. They had just got the confirmation of the one animal being positive — it had been doubtful on the first test. Therefore, because of contiguous contagion, we are facing into a régime of very frequent tests. There was some talk of every two months. And it isn't just the immediate farms, but quite a wide ring all around here will face that. The Department official wanted to know precisely how many animals were nearby at the time. He appeared to be more concerned over our heifers than our cows, and they, fortunately, had paddocks stopped for silage between them and possible infection. However, the fact that we are autumn calving is very bad since they are now at their most vulnerable stage. And we never had a better lot of in-calf heifers, all bred to AI with synchronised mating. This is our very first time doing that and only the other day we were commenting what nice little udders they were making already. Now the big fear will be if they start bagging up too quickly. We will have to watch them like hawks from now on. Isolation of anything even remotely suspicious is going to be the order of the day around this place until this scare is over.

Our only hope is that this was just an isolated case that

our neighbour had and that it hasn't spread to the rest of his herd. That has just been tested so it will take at least ten days before our worst fears can be dispelled or realised. If this test is negative, and remains negative, we will have an excellent chance of escaping infection. All this information I related to Eoin, as a form of consolation, since he nearly hit the roof when he first heard the news. The boys did not seem to grasp the awfulness of the situation quite as clearly. But Eoin and I have already lived through a brucellosis storm, in the bad old days, and it is something you wouldn't wish on your worst enemy.

We had a perfectly clear herd until the awful day, in the mid-1960s, when we went to a farm dispersal sale of pedigree cows and bought two animals. We were desperate to build up our numbers and the quality of our animals, but the prices were too high for our meagre pocket. The two we bought were oldish cows. Still, as they were in calf we thought that at least we had a nucleus to start with, and great was our delight when they each produced a heifer calf. But those were the most expensive calves that anybody ever got. What we did not find out until too late — when our own animals were aborting left right and centre — was that the herd was being sold off in its entirety because of bad brucellosis.

We should have known better, of course. The clues had been there for us if we had only had the wit to read them. Practically every animal in that sale had a copper wire stuck through its dewlap. When we inquired why, from the owner, we were told that it was an old pishogue, to keep disease away. We smiled at each other, in a superior way, as we did at the sight of the goat running with the herd. It was only when it was too late that we realised the significance of both the copper wires and the goat. Both were seen as preventatives of brucellosis. Don't ask me how either was supposed to work. All I can tell you is that our first abortions started that year, and went on for many a long year. That farmer must be roasting in hell, if curses have any power at all, because he was well and truly cursed for what he did to us, young and innocent as we were at the time. And of course he spread disease to a lot more than us, as we were only one of the many buyers that day.

'No man is an island,' said the poet Donne long and merry ago, and that is more true for farmers than for anyone else. No farm is an island. What happens on one farm impinges on all around. That is as true today as in the 1960s when we personally, unwittingly, brought brucellosis into this area. Then there was no such thing as compulsory brucellosis testing. But there is today. So how did it get here? That is the question we are all asking. The rumours are flying but, please God, the infection is not.

AUGUST

Another Poor Woman's Son

I had to laugh this morning — or I would have laughed if I had dared. I just about managed to keep the laughter in until Eoin and I could enjoy the joke together, all on our own. You see, when I got up to the milking parlour this morning, this son of mine came up out of the pit like an avenging angel. He then waded into the attack without as much as a 'Hello' or a 'Good morning, Mother'.

'Where were you last night?' he demanded to know. 'Who did you go out with? When was that arranged? Why didn't you leave us a note...?' The questions came faster than my answers, and he had a face on him that would stop a clock. The cows also skeetered off out the yard in fright at the cross tone of voice. And, as I said, I was afraid to laugh because I knew that that would have infuriated him entirely. But I was so sorely tempted to give him a taste of his own medicine. I'm really sorry now that I didn't just say 'Out' and turn on my heel and leave.

Time and again that's what the same fellow has said and done to me and he off out the back door. Any further questioning never elicited any further information. I might, at a push, get 'Just out...' — two words instead of the one, and neither conveying any real information. Of course, I could see he was on his way out. But if I hadn't seen him, I wouldn't even know he was gone out until I noticed the car gone.

That was my son's problem last night. He came home and there was no sign of our car. I'd safely say he wasn't too early himself and he must have been really worried about us because didn't he ring some of our closest friends, getting them out of bed, to ask were we there. Finally, it appears, he fell asleep, on top of his bed, while listening and waiting for us to come home — which we duly did quite unaware of the commotion we had inadvertently caused. That's why he was attacking me — because I forgot to tell him that we would be out late last night. Talk about the boot being on the other foot!

Some day last week we were asked out to dinner, and I could swear I told him about it as I came off the phone. But it often happens that I forget which son I've told my bit of news to. Then, if I go and tell the same one all over again, I get attacked for going on and on about small things. And even if I tell the son I hadn't told before, but he has already heard it from his brother, I'm quickly told that he already knows that, and I find nothing so deflating as being told, 'I know that already', when I am full of some little bit of news. It shuts me up on the spot.

Now, it isn't only my sons who deflate me like that. There are some people I can never tell anything to because, as sure as sure, my information will be greeted with something like 'Don't the dogs going the road know that already?'

Conversation, I always tell my sons, is like a tennis game. You are supposed to hit the ball back and not kill it stone dead. They take not a blind bit of notice of me, however. I still get the monosyllabic 'Out', when I am just trying to make pleasant conversation as they pass me by on their way to the door. But maybe the tone of my voice betrays my real feelings, when I see them heading out the door at the time we were afraid to come in at. There are no Cinderellas around any more, it seems, whose parents insist that their daughters keep decent hours. Times sure have changed.

Yet some things never change. I met a woman during the

week whose son had just crashed the family car. She was one angry lady, as she explained all about it, while I gave her and her boxes a spin home from the Country Market. The cost of the repairs was killing her. Needless to say, there was no comprehensive cover while the son drove. Fortunately, however, he had just walked away from the crash. 'But he could have been killed stone dead,' she went on. 'And if I could only lay my hands on whoever was driving that car in the middle of the road and never dimmed his lights ... his mother wouldn't recognise him by the time I'd be done. Blind drunk I suppose the b-----d was (excuse my French, Liz). But wouldn't you think the guards would catch the likes of them? But oh no. They are never where they should be. So that bloody b-----d was able to drive on, even though he must have known he had driven my poor Paddy into the ditch.'

'Hold on a minute,' I wanted to say, if only I could have got a word in edgeways. I could smell a rat before she was even half-way launched into her story. The phantom car was striking again without even the grace of a variation or two. That very same driver had 'dyked' two of my sons on that very same twisty bit of the road. The time 'he' had caused our car to be turned upside down, however, 'he' was on a motorbike. That motorcyclist didn't have the grace to stop either. He was going too fast anyway, we were told. And not one of my sons was ever able to get a licence number of the vehicle at fault.

We swallowed the yarn completely the first time we heard it. I mean, our eldest son told it so convincingly. And our sons just did not lie to us, no matter what! Ah well, five sons later, and many, many crashes, even the most doting of parents would begin to doubt their sons' veracity. Somehow or other there was always that driver who never stopped. The odd thing, however, was that there was never a brake mark left on the road, and surely he must have braked some bit when my sons hove into view. Neither could we ever find a bit of contrasting paint on our damaged vehicles. When we changed our colour of car, so too, obviously, did the phantom driver.

But what are any of us to do when our sons swear blind that that's what happened? They were there; we weren't. And they do lie so convincingly. Even Pádraig, the most inventive of them all, just couldn't be shaken in his story of that woman, with the child in the pram, who was there, slap-bang in the middle of the road, when he came around the corner.

'Now, Mom, even you wouldn't have me kill a young mother and her child so as to save the car?' he said calculatingly. 'I had no choice but to head sideways for the ditch....'

'And was she grateful to you?' I enquired, sarcasm dripping like treacle.

'No, Mom! Now that was the really odd thing. She ran off down the road, back the way she had come.' He answered with such a straight face that I knew there was no point in asking him just what was a woman doing, out with a child in a pram, after midnight, on a quiet country road. It was only when we went up to rescue the Landrover that we saw just why she had run back down the road — there was no room for even a pram to pass the crashed vehicle.

Pádraig obviously had time to plan his story well before he came creeping into our room to whisper, 'Dad, Dad.' This wasn't the first night by any means that we had been woken by such a whisper. Too many times by far, each of them had crept into our room, in the middle of the night, when they were in trouble. I wonder where did the phantom driver go for help? I do hope he had understanding parents as well!

Harvest Straw

The corn is still being cut all around us at the moment with the first of the spring-sown barley ripe. And there are smiles all around since moisture is as low as 16 per cent, and reported yields well over the two tonnes, pushing the three tonnes at times. That is excellent for spring-sown grain. We don't grow grain any more but it is always great to see fellow farmers doing well. Of course, the price of straw does hit us since we buy in straw every year. But I still think it is great to see the lorry-loads of straw passing the main road at the bottom of our hill, several times a day. It is only a few years ago that the sight around here at this time of the year was fields of straw being torched since nobody wanted it. This is a grain-growing area with relatively few farmers in cows.

I still find it hard to come to terms with the bulk of the harvest being all over in high summer, when in the past it would be just beginning. Harvest was the end of the summer. Now, mid-August and all our straw is home. Of course, it is all so much easier now with big bales and the tractors doing all the handling. But I am wondering if there will be much straw for me in my garden with the price of it this year. There does seem to be a greater effort going on at storing it away safely — normally you would find bales lost at the side of the roads and nobody bothering to pick them up. I often stopped myself and threw one into the jeep, just so that they would not be wasted. Not one bale like that, however, have I seen this year. On the home front, I wanted some big bales brought down to the garden for spreading later on when they would be nicely softened up by the rain which surely will come by then. But I didn't get them. So I must wait for my straw until the calving starts and I get the once-used straw from the calving pens.

I am planning a greater-than-ever usage this year because

we have a marvellous potato crop. Last March, when all the cajoling in the world failed to get my vegetable ground prepared for me, I gave up and planted my early potatoes straight into the uncultivated and winter weedy ground. I just stuck down my spade and slipped in a potato behind it. Then I came around one of the lads to deliver me down a load of strawy dung from the calf pens, and they dumped it all over my potato plot. Once the tractor could drive over the ground, they had no objection. It is any hand-work in the garden they really hate, and the dung was in their way anyway where it was.

So Eoin and I spread the stuff all over my potatoes, about six inches deep in places. Eoin was sort of an unwilling helper, because he said that the potatoes would never come up through that, and I think he also likes the look of the potato drills all freshly ridged up. But I argued that they come up through hard soil, so why would they not grow up through easy straw? And I was right. The potatoes were never so good or so easy. No earthing up, no weeding — all we had to do was spray and dig them. But the extraordinary thing is that the potatoes all seem to form between the earth and the straw. So digging is dead simple. It mainly consists of pushing aside the straw and picking up beautifully clean potatoes, and not a sun-greened one among them. I planted my winter broccoli and cabbage through the now brittle straw where the early rows were. And I had hardly a weed to pull. Since three households are now digging my potatoes, the ground will be ready soon too for the spring cabbage plants, which I sowed last week.

That's the card I must use next time I want help in the garden, because my city daughters-in-law do seem to appreciate the ready availability of fruit and vegetables — even though I swear that they, like their husbands, are convinced that such things just grow of their own accord. Wait until they're trying to grow them themselves, is what I say to myself when their easy acceptance of all my hard work irks. I have yet to see any one of the four of them do so much as pull a weed. They just help themselves, without comment, to the produce. So you can understand just why it is that I am trying to discover the easiest ways of growing all my fruit and vegetables. And the liberal use of straw, in any form I can get it, is the answer. Every year I am trying it somewhere new.

Another success story this year was the asparagus. That was also covered, six inches deep, with strawy dung from the calf pens, and we never had better asparagus. I have always grown this luxury vegetable but it was never a great favourite in this house — young peas and beans and carrots being the preferred choices. That was before I discovered the microwave for it. I had got Darina Allen's book on vegetable cooking and she suggested baking asparagus with a trace of oil and a grind of sea-salt — which is fine if one has an oven on. So, instead, I put a serving of asparagus on a plate — just the tender tops where they snap off easily — dotted it with butter, and one grind of sea-salt, covered it with cling-wrap, and put it for five minutes in the microwave. It turned out only gorgeous, a real, strong asparagus taste, which you lose when you steam or boil the tips in water. With fresh bread to mop up the buttery juices it made many a supper for Eoin and myself this summer. I wouldn't waste it on the rest of them. Let them make their own discoveries.

Breast is Best

All last week, Michaella couldn't wait for her school to re-open. One of the many wet evenings was spent covering her new school books. I remember doing the exact same long ago with the brown paper that always came with any shopping and was carefully stored by my mother for further use. There was an art to mitring the corners properly and also to cutting out the U-shape for folding back behind the spines of the bigger books. Sara is a past master at the task, but now with colourful wrapping paper specially bought for the job, and the ever-useful sellotape. Thus, the school bag was packed in readiness days in advance, as Michaella counted off the hours before she'd see all her friends again.

This is a big year for Michaella, going into first class in school. She is no longer an infant. And, as proof positive, she has just lost the first of her top front teeth. My little girl is rapidly disappearing on me, even though the tooth fairy duly called. Her gap-toothed smile at what she got under her pillow showed both her delight and her innocence. These are the little things that make childhood so special, even though some purists say that even this — like Santa — is a form of deceit. Lord preserve us from extremists on either side is all I say.

There have been so many letters to the papers recently on this new Relationships and Sexuality Education (RSE) pro-gramme, for national schools, that I got hold of the full interim RSE curriculum and guidelines for primary schools because I was curious to find out the ins and outs of this much-discussed programme. And now that I've read it, I can't for the life of me understand what all the fuss is about, including all the anti-letters to the papers every second day.

I'll tell you this much. I can find nothing wrong in giving children the proper words to discuss feelings, emotions and bodily parts and functions, and thus to remove the unease and downright embarrassment they can feel about quite normal parts of life. When I was young, we were trained at home to say that we needed to do 'something', when we wanted to go to the toilet. And, for years afterwards, when-ever the word 'something' came into normal conversation, which of course it frequently did, I would nearly die of embarrassment and blush violently. I was into my teens before I could use the word with any ease or comfort.

Children, I find, take everything for normal. A friend

visited lately with her six-month-old baby who she breast-fed very openly indeed. And, next day, both granddaughters were breastfeeding their dolls here as part of their play. While being highly amused, I was very careful at the same time not to pass any comment except to tell them that I fed their Daddy too, just like that, when he was my baby. I think it is important that they should think this is a perfectly normal function, even at this young age. I only hope I live to see them breastfeeding my great-grandchildren.

And then, while all this was going on, one of the funny incidents of my breastfeeding days came back into my mind with the realisation that somewhere in the world there is a thirty-three-year-old man who was once breast fed by me. I don't even know his name. All I know is that he and Pádraig were both born in early August in a certain maternity hospital.

This time I had a private room, complete with television. At that time we stayed in hospital for a full week after the birth. Towards the end of my stay, the nurse brought in my baby, as usual, to be fed at two o'clock. I had just had a good lunch, and I was watching an old film on the television. With the ease of experience, the fourth time around, I put the baby to the breast where he suckled lustily as usual, and I relaxed in comfort, propped up by pillows, soothed by the voice of Charles Boyar and the old romantic values on the television screen.

The baby was just about finishing off the second side when the door burst open and the same nurse was back, wheeling another cot and another crying baby. She literally grabbed the now replete child from my breast and said that it wasn't mine at all. Would you believe that I had fed the wrong baby and just hadn't noticed the difference? I had even changed his nappy when he noisily and noisomely filled it while he sucked.

The other mother, in the room next door, was more ob-servant, however. She was bottle feeding, like every other mother in the hospital that time. My child was sound asleep when he was wheeled in to her and she hadn't woken him up to feed him. But when she did, he flatly refused the proffered bottle and protested strongly. Then she spotted the wrong name on his wristband, confirmed by the blue-bordered card on the cot. This much information I got from the worried nurse while that child was being tucked back into his cot and I was given Pádraig and a bottle, doubtless the same one he had already refused.

Then the nurse was gone, with all evidence of the baby I had briefly wet-nursed. I didn't even get to read his surname. But somewhere he is walking around, completely oblivious of our brief special relationship. I bet he would have died of embarrassment when he was a youngster if he had met me and known what he and I had done. I doubt if even the RSE programme would cover that situation.

Funeral Plans

Well now, it is all discussed and decided — what Eoin and I would like done when our day comes, as come it must. But did I ever think I would see the day when I would seriously sit down and thrash out what I would like, and what I would definitely not like, at my funeral? Yet Eoin and myself, when we finally got home from his cousin's funeral, talked in the most natural way possible, and in the whole of our health, of the day which must inevitably come. Now, all that is left for me is to go the full hog and write everything down — all we agreed — and seal it in an envelope inscribed in big bold capitals:

NOT TO BE OPENED UNTIL AFTER MY DEATH

Eoin was really funny, and sad as well, as he told me of how things were when he first came to live here — how his uncle had left precisely such an envelope, covering precise details down to the room in the house in which he wanted to be laid out, where he wanted to be buried, who was to dig the grave and who he wanted to shoulder the coffin. The stipends to the priests and altar boys were also stipulated, as was the inscription to be put on the gravestone exactly twelve months later. Nothing was forgotten.

I remember once, when I wasn't long married, reading that letter and thinking how morbid the man must have been, planning his funeral in such detail. But I did have the good sense to keep the letter. And now, on re-reading it, I am beginning to think instead how eminently sensible that uncle was.

Eoin, while we were doing our forward planning, also looked back at how good the cousin, whose funeral we had just attended, had been to him in the early years, and he was really sad at his passing. It seemed to ease his pain to tell again, in detail, of how he would never have been able to hang onto this farm if it hadn't been for this particular cousin.

Eoin, as I have told you before, did not grow up on this farm, but inherited it from an unmarried uncle, who didn't have a lot of choice since Eoin was the only male child, in the one and only family from the five brothers and one sister in his father's family. So this particular branch of the Kavanaghs hung by a very slender line indeed, with Eoin having no first cousins from his father's side. But he had a lot of second cousins of the name, because his grandfather's eldest brother bred a much more prolific lot, many of whom stayed farming in the parish.

'Weren't you the lucky one then, inheriting a fine farm?' is a comment often made to Eoin. But Eoin's inheritance was one horse, the implements to go with same, one house cow and three bullocks. There were over a hundred acres of land all right, but the banks had a decided first claim on that, and those few animals that were there had free range through the furze and scrub.

So, of course, everybody knew that Eoin would have to sell. Indeed, offers for parts of his inheritance came in indecently quickly, which is another tale worth telling. But this merely strengthened Eoin's resolve to make a go of it, come hell or high water, although he really knew little about farming and had absolutely no money, nor much hope of raising any with the debts he also inherited.

And hell it soon appeared it would be, when, one week after his uncle's death, that one horse died. It died of tetanus actually. But all the old people around just nodded their heads and said that the horse always died after the master. But this horse was to be Eoin's sole means of getting in some fields of grain, and a field of sugar beet. So he really was facing disaster.

But then, on the death of the horse, his second cousin, and near neighbour, stepped in, and advised him to sell the few bullocks and to grow grain on every acre he could plough on the place, and a field of sugar beet too if he could manage it. Still, what's more to the point, he offered Eoin his own tractor and all his implements in order that Eoin could do so. Joe also went surety for the seed money.

So, every night, when Joe finished his own work and went to his supper at about half past six, Eoin would go over for the tractor and work the night through, and have the tractor back in Joe's yard before eight o'clock in the morning. Not alone that, but Joe always had the fuel tank of the tractor full to the brim each and every evening when Eoin went over, knowing full well that there was no way Eoin could return it in the same condition.

His help went even further because, that first night with the tractor and plough, nothing would do Eoin, with malice aforethought, but to start work on a bawn field, in full view of the all the neighbours, to show that he was going to hang on to his farm. And, of course, to his utter mortification, he couldn't manage, no matter what he did, to set the plough right. If he had known enough to go into one of the two

small stubble fields, which was all his uncle, in his state of
health, could then cultivate with his one horse, he'd have
had some chance of success.

Finally he had to go and ask his cousin if he'd ever leave
his comfortable fireside and his new bride, to come over and
show himself how to plough — which he did, in the spring
moonlight. That year, thanks to Joe, Eoin got in a hundred
acres of grain, on what was virtually virgin soil, and had a
wonderful harvest because 1955 was also a very good grain
year. And out of it Eoin was able to buy his own tractor and
plough, and hold on to his land. I think the notion may even
have taken him then that it was high time he got himself a
wife, and that's why he still says he fell in love at first sight
when we met just a few short months later.

But that's another story. This week Joe died and Eoin is
full of memories and sorrow that he never really said just how
much he owed to a good man — his cousin and neighbour.

SEPTEMBER

Bad Rearing

I started thinking about life today at dinner time, and asking questions. This is a dangerous enough occupation at the best of times since you may not like the answers you come up with. The main question exercising my mind today was, why have I missed out on having the breast of the chicken at both ends of my life? It just isn't fair. I know only too well that life isn't fair. But my generation, so far, got it at neither end.

We had roast chicken today for dinner, with stuffing, our own potatoes and not alone cauliflower fresh from the garden, but also garden peas, frozen by me, at the peak of their perfection. So, with all the rest of the trimmings, and apple tart and custard to follow, I felt that, for once, I had outdone myself and there should be no complaints this dinner-time.

Eoin, bless him, will eat everything put in front of him, without complaint. But the lads are a totally different matter. 'Resurrection Day again, folks...' is the kindest of the comments I have to put up with if using leftovers in any way. 'Bad rearing,' I can almost hear my mother saying at such times. And, true enough, those sons of ours don't seem to know when they are well off.

They have no idea of what a rare treat roast chicken was to my own family when we were growing up. My eldest brother used to joke that when we had chicken for dinner either one of us, or the chicken, was sick. And he wasn't far wrong. The cockerels from the clutch were raised for sale and the pullets for future laying. But if anything went wrong with one of them, we ate it. And, should one of us be sick, the best spared fowl, of either sex, was turned into chicken broth to give us strength in our convalescence.

That could have been an old bird. Yet we also ate chickens when they were at a totally uneconomic young age. If anybody is old enough to remember the awful, soul-destroying job of training chickens to perch at night, and how they would crowd and smother each other if the job of perching them was left even ten minutes too late at dusk, they may also remember very young chicken for dinner the following day. Sweet eating they were too, at one per person.

My parents had gone through the economic war and all that entailed. So waste of any kind was not allowed. It really was subsistence farming long before that term was ever invented. We had our own bacon, our own eggs and occasional chickens to eat. We made our own butter and used lots of cream and buttermilk in our daily diet. We grew all our own potatoes and vegetables. We never bought baker's bread and made our own white flour during the war years — even when that was strictly illegal. Sausages and black puddings were made after the killing of the pig, and life was altogether much simpler.

My father sat at the head of the table and carved. He distributed the white and dark meat precisely as he saw fit, and never once asked us for our preference. Indeed, he also had the power to wither us with a look. Eoin says that his house was exactly the same. We never dared object to any decision of our parents. They had spoken and that was that. We obeyed and kept our feelings to ourselves. In short, the fathers' authority was epitomised by that formal carving of meat while sitting at the head of the table.

How different it was here this dinner-time. The boys came in first. I think one of them did say, 'Oh good! Roast chicken!' Then, while I was dishing up the vegetables, those sons proceeded to divide up the breast meat between them and help themselves to the stuffing and roast potatoes.

When Eoin came in, a trifle late I grant you, and I got his plate ready for him, it struck me very forcibly how things had changed in just one generation. We would never have dreamed of starting a meal until my father was first seated. But my lot were hard at it when Eoin sat down, and I don't know if they even acknowledged his presence. Nor did they seem aware that there was no white meat and little stuffing left for their father or me. And neither did either of us make any complaint: we had perfectly good dinners from what was left.

The order of preference has shifted quite drastically. In so many homes the children now come first, with the father second, and mother making do with what is left. I sometimes term myself the dustbin as I rescue discarded food from my sons' side-plates, discarded, without qualm, because of the slightest trace of fat. They don't like me doing that, and tell me so. If I justify my action by talking of the cost of meat today, I am told that this is the 1980s and to stop going on and on about small things. In other words, I am to stop nagging.

That is the crux of the problem. Not alone has my generation missed out on having the breast meat of the chicken by right; we have also never had a time to be right without question. Our parents were always right and never tolerated a word of complaint from any of their children. Indeed, no matter what we thought, or how things might be festering inside, we never dared voice our feelings, not even in those turbulent teenage years.

And now that we are parents of grown-up children ourselves, it is we who are half afraid to express our true feelings lest we cause a row. Our children have no such inhibitions. God knows, I have been told of my most annoying faults and mannerisms, often enough and loudly enough, over the years. The latest tirade was that I shouldn't scratch my bum, '*ever*!' Where, oh where, have I gone wrong?

Or have I gone wrong at all? I may be regularly told to stop nagging, or scratching my bottom absent-mindedly. I may never get the coveted breast meat of the roast chicken. My sons, however, tell me things that neither Eoin nor I would ever have dreamt of discussing with our parents. We hear all the latest jokes going the rounds, whether they are about moving statues or sexual peccadilloes. I've noticed Eoin getting strategically deaf at times so as not to laugh aloud. And, best of all, I do love it when they say, 'Do you know what happened last night, Mom?'

Then I immediately down tools and stop whatever it is I'm doing, to hear all, or at least a lot, about the current girlfriend and her family, or about friends and their families. We find our sons all chat much more freely to me than they do to their father. But I suppose this is because we have all boys. Do girls tend to confide more in their fathers at this stage?

So now, do you think my sons are badly reared and should I stake our claim to the breast of the next chicken I roast? Or is it all too late? Should I adopt the following motto I once saw on the back of a car?

Don't get mad — get even ...
Live long enough to be a burden on your children.

Maybe, as a visiting Granny, I may yet get the breast meat on my plate. Or, better again, Eoin and I could do ourselves real well, food-wise, when there are only the two of us to cook for and forget all about saving for the next generation. Let them support us for a change. I also wonder who in the as-yet-unborn third generation will get the breast meat. I have a sneaking suspicion that then there'll be no losers, because there'll be nothing but breast fillets bought when it comes to buying chicken. What my mother would consider a mortal sin, I a waste, they will consider one of the necessities of life.

Battle Lines in the Kitchen

Quite a discussion started in my kitchen this week over a cup of tea and cake when a group of our women's club met here for our first committee meeting under my chairmanship. Now, I had no notion of having the tea in the kitchen for the simple reason that it was a cup in the hand for everybody in all the other houses. So we had conducted the main business of the morning in my sitting-room all right, where I even had a fire going and fresh flowers all over the place.

Yet, when I went out to the kitchen to make the expected cup of tea, first one woman followed me out. Then another came. And, finally, before the kettle was well boiled, they were all in my kitchen. So we finished up having the tea there as well, and not 'in state' inside as I had planned.

Strange how everybody always finishes up in the kitchen in my house, no matter what the occasion, and be they young or old. I know it's the biggest room in the house, with plenty of room for everybody. After all, I am well used to feeding all and sundry as well as my own crew. We only just finished the last lot of silage this week and I found I had thirteen extra in to both dinner and tea that day because somebody in the silage circus had brought their children along as well for the outing, and they were the first to sit down at my table. I wasn't best pleased you may be sure. But there was no way out of it but to make my own family do without.

Silage harvesting comes but twice a year. But at least twice a week here it can be hard-going for Eoin and myself to get into our own kitchen for our going-to-bed cup of tea, with the bodies of the sons' friends draped all over the place. I am strongly thinking of investing in an electric kettle for the bedroom just like you find in some hotels. It would be handy too for if ever I'm sick. Actually, come to think of it, it would be handier still if one of those girls cluttering up the place at night proves to be the woman who permanently takes over my kitchen. But I don't have to worry about that quite yet.

I was given something to worry about, however, when one of my friends picked up my container of Premarin pills from where they always stay by my place at the kitchen table. Otherwise I'd be bound to forget my morning dose of oestrogen.

'Are you still on those, Liz?' she asked. 'Don't you know that they are particularly hard on the liver and you really should have changed over to the patch long ago?'

I don't know what made her so wise as she has had no medical training, no more than myself. But she was very definite indeed on the subject, and even lifted her blouse to show us a small, clear circle of what looked like cellophane, stuck onto her side. I had often heard talk and jokes about 'the patch'. But this was my first time actually seeing one, and *in situ* as well. I had had an idea that it was some kind of an implant — a major sort of a job — and foolishly enough said so, to her great amusement.

'I just stick another one on, twice a week,' she informed us. 'It never comes off in the bath. The only problem can be from too much friction.' So, half boasting, she explained why she had it stuck where it was, out of the way of everything.

'But what's it all for, at the heel of the hunt?' then asked another woman. 'You're all going to look old eventually. So why do you go to all that bother and expense? A woman of fifty-five just doesn't look anything like a woman of twenty-five, no matter what she does — nor should she expect to...'

And there and then, the battle lines were drawn: those, myself included, who were all for anything that would make us feel better, look younger, and have enough energy to keep going; the other vociferous minority holding the view that it was all wrong to go against nature, nobody knew what the long-term effects would be, and we would all — the lot of us on oestrogen — finish up with huge breasts.

'Better than having them hanging down to your waist, or

withered away to nothing,' retorted my know-all friend, without giving the other side a proper chance to finish their argument. As I said, the battle lines were really drawn. The arguments were inclined to be a bit on the hot side because both the pro- and the anti- camps seemed to be extremely defensive on the subject and operating the attack-is-the-best-method-of-defence approach. Me? I just listened on and got educated. I was quite unaware that Premarin pills are made from the urine of pregnant mares who roam the prairies in Canada with catheters attached to great big urine sacks!

Where would we be without our women friends to keep us in touch with what is actually happening in the world, be it true or false? I know we read a lot about such matters in the various publications. But that is not the same as having the whole issue thrashed out in front of you and hearing the real personal experiences of people. The known true facts we can separate ourselves from the hearsay, the word of authority figures in the speaker's life.

'My doctor never recommended me to have any of this hormone messing around. And John always says that he is a very sound man,' then chimed in one of the anti- camp, as though that should finish the discussion on the spot. Her tone of voice, even more than her words, reminded me, all of a sudden, of years ago when that same woman regularly made a laughing stock of herself by trotting out her husband's words, always prefaced by 'John says', as though absolutely everything John said was gospel and therefore must be true. While we may have been all a little inclined that way, ourselves, when first married, she just took the biscuit. It is common enough for starry-eyed young brides, even today, to quote their husbands as if they were the fountain of all wisdom. But time usually cures them of that notion when they learn that their man isn't always right and they begin to stand on their own two feet.

Yet here was this middle-aged woman evidently still needing a male authority figure whose mere word sufficed.

She was quite unable to explain to us why HRT was contra-indicated in her case. She'd never asked her doctor, she said. Still, she must have asked him something because it is my experience that you only get what you look for from doctors. Very few that I ever heard of suggest HRT, out of the blue, for any menopausal woman. The woman, herself, must first request it, even if in a roundabout fashion. Then, and only then, will it be prescribed for her. That's how I first got a prescription for Premarin at any rate, and it has been renewed only at my specific request.

You know how when we bring our cars to the garage for their regular service and each time a label is hung on the steering-wheel rod, when we return to collect it, telling us that the next service is due at x miles on the clock. Should not we too, when we go to our doctor, have a total check-over and then be told to return at six months, a year or whatever? Lest I forget, perhaps a label around my neck, stating that my next check-up should be at age sixty, might be a good idea. Or a card in the post, such as my optician and dentist send, might spur me into action, especially if then I'd be automatically given the benefit of whatever new technology had come in the meantime.

My American son, on his usual long call home during the week, mentioned in passing that he had just had his compulsory annual check-up and it was all systems go. The company he works for insists that all its employees have this, and, what's more, that they then carry out the company doctor's order, that is if they want to keep their jobs. Here, we'd probably have actions for unfair dismissal or invasion of privacy.

Anyway, after that frank discussion in my kitchen, for fear of the fears, I went to my doctor and asked should I, at my age, be on the patch instead of the pill. The net result of that consultation is that I am now experimenting where to place the patch on my body. So, no doubt, I'll let you know what ensues.

Letting Off Steam

Do you know, but sometimes I think my main function here is to act as a safety valve? The steam, the hot air, the fire, is supposed to go through me, the mother, with no damage to me either mentally or physically. At least that is how my menfolk behave.

People quite frequently ask us how it is that Eoin and his two sons get on so well together when other fathers and sons, and indeed brothers too, would willingly gut each other. Now, it is not always all sweetness and light here either, especially on days like today. But there has never been a row over something serious. It is always over something small and often stupid as well, like who should have checked that the fencing was okay before cattle were moved into a field.

That was the big complaint today and I knew something was wrong when I saw one son heading determinedly over to me in the orchard. I dread seeing the black faces coming to me, wherever I am, with trouble writ large on their countenances. I brace myself for the complaint, whatever it is, and try either to make placatory remarks, coming down on no one side, or, if I can see clearly where the fault lies, saying so regardless. Then that son goes away either quite happy having been vindicated or in an even worse temper, saying that I always back the other fellow anyway. I am lucky if that is not made retrospective way back to their earliest childhood. But I know quite well that they are only letting off steam and it is better letting it off harmlessly, through me in the garden, than having a head-to-head confrontation in the yard, when real harm could be done.

Because, regardless of what they, or their wives, may think, none of my sons are perfect, nor Eoin either for that matter. He also comes to let off steam on occasions and it is doubly important that he is able to do so safely. I must say, he has been a marvellous father, always giving his sons great freedom and autonomy. But he can be very cross indeed over small things, like the free electricity he always says that we must have here, as he keeps turning off lights, all over the place. And missing tools drive him especially wild when he needs a particular socket set, right this minute, and that precise one is the only one missing out of the box. Of course, nobody, but nobody, took it or has the faintest notion where it is. The other bane of his life, which is pertinent to today's problem, is the fact that he just can't get them to test the shock properly, in the electric fences, each and every time that they put animals in a field, and also to check the shock again on the daily rounds.

'I don't care if it was perfect yesterday or even this morning,' is all he says to them. But to me he lets off steam about how he must have shown them, and told them, a million and one times, to go down on one knee and test the wire with a piece of grass — but no, they just won't do that. They barely put one wire against another and then listen for the click. Or, the few times that they do use the grass method, they never go down on one knee but stay standing and so can't judge the strength of the shock because their wellingtons insulate them. Or, which is the nub of the problem, he knows full well that they never test it at all, just presume it is right, because they hate getting the shock.

I make suitable noises while all this steam is being left off and try to say the right thing to Eoin. After all, it is they, themselves, who will have all the bother of rounding up the animals if they do break out. But I may as well be idle for all the good that soft answer does me. I make Eoin even crosser because don't I know quite well that that is not the way it should be done? There is a grazing rotation that must be followed, religiously, and it is stupid things like that which cause the whole system to break down. And how can he take no notice when so much depends on things going right, and so on and so on and so forth?

So, do you see what I mean when I say that it is not always

easy going here? Problems do arise. You know that you can foresee the big problems and legislate against them — like ensuring that nobody takes even £1 more out of the common purse than anybody else. And that means us as well as them. What each partner does, then, with their money, is precisely their own affair. I may lift an eyebrow to myself at times but I have no right to say anything. All major farm decisions, however, are discussed and agreed by all four of us.

Eoin and I are very much active partners — mentally if not quite so much physically any more. But, in a way, that is a blessing. The old folk should not interfere in the day-to-day running of the farm by the younger men. That is the main problem when fathers come along and countermand the decisions of their sons. I have heard that complaint umpteen times from sons and even more so from their wives, when they'd be telling me of their problems. Then, I might hear their fathers and mothers, in turn, saying that they just have to take control at times, that it is all right for us to be talking, but their sons want to do the most stupid things from time to time. However, who is to say what is daft, or not, until it is tried and tested? And if it is daft, the sons are the ones who will suffer most if the parents never ever pick up the pieces when something does go wrong.

We work here on a three-way split, each household getting precisely the same profit share. So, if they do themselves well financially, so do we. But if they make mistakes, they suffer more proportionally, in the resultant loss, because their needs are greater than ours right now. They want everything, starting off in life as they are, while we want for nothing really, beyond the food on our table.

Yet we don't make things easy for them. We always take our full rightful share, regardless. What they want they have to earn or borrow for themselves. And, if they have the notion that they would do better on their own, without the three-way split, which, needless to say, has been suggested, we simply say, 'Fine. You each take your share of the profits which have accrued since starting, in kind. We will rent one, or both, of you the land at the going rate. The same will apply to the quota and our share of the cows and machinery. Then we will sit back and live very comfortably indeed. Or, alternatively, get that same money by renting to an outsider.'

That softens their cough for them very fast indeed. They don't need a calculator to reckon the economic answer.

There now, I have just let off steam about them letting off steam.

Pumpkins and Farming

Today, Sunday, I wrote my granddaughters' names on two of my biggest pumpkins, and they were all excitement at the thought of their names growing every day with the pumpkins. At least, Michaella was all excitement. Nicole just tags along.

Michaella told me that they, and their mother, had brought in the cows for their Daddy before they came over to me. That was a very long walk for small legs. But I do love to see them involved in anything to do with farming, and to see their mother involved as well.

I have a pet theory that unless children get involved with farming at a very young age, when they are at their most impressionable stage, you are lessening your chances considerably of them wanting anything to do with farming when they grow older. Now, it is all great fun for the granddaughters, helping Daddy. But they are also getting the message, loud and clear, that it is okay to do this kind of work. Once they get out into the wider world, they will be bombarded with subliminal messages about farming not being okay, especially for girls.

Ideally, of course, they should be helping Mammy as well as Daddy. Now, that is what I would really like to see happening in my family — perhaps because that was the way it was with my sons. When they came milking the cows with me, they were helping me, full stop. Their Daddy was usually doing tractor-work somewhere else. They rarely went with him because we were very slow, always, about letting them, as children, have hand, act or part with farm machinery. It is just too dangerous: You can't watch children around machinery.

But our sons were used to cows almost from the word go. Our very first milking parlour — a three-unit chute — had a much-too-wide pit, for the very simple reason that we dug outside the lines marking out the foundations, when we were meant to dig inside them. That will tell you how long ago that was, because we knew no better, and that pit was dug out by hand, with a pick and shovel. I cannot recall whether it was to save money, or because there was no such thing as a JCB in those days. I got fine welts on my hands at the time, if I remember correctly.

The plans we were given, for our edifice, were sketchy, to say the least. But, as so often happens in life, that mistake of an over-wide pit proved a godsend to a working mother. It was wide enough to fit a tea chest and still leave me room to operate. So, the baby — when it was one baby — was placed in that, as in a cot, and the high solid sides protected him from splashes of cow dung or wash water.

As he grew, it acted as a playpen. And, in due course, another tea chest appeared in the parlour pit. I can't say that I finished up with five tea chests in a row, to match my sons. But I do remember doubling up the occupants at times.

Then — it now seems all too quickly — those sons were helping to milk the cows. Seamus particularly tugs at my heart-strings. My abiding memory of him is with his little wooden box, which he always carried around with him to stand on, so that he could reach the cows' udders to put on the units.

It was only three units after all, so there must have been time to give him time. It would be a very different story if Michaella were to try to milk in the milking parlour of today when it is all speed and throughput of cows per hour.

But I'll tell you something that hasn't changed in the least, in a generation, and that is thought given to working wives with children, by milking-parlour designers. These, of course, are all men. We are building a new milking parlour at the moment on the outside farm, because the two brothers want to diversify a little. They have been working together now, in the one herd, for over ten years. And, in a way, they are cramping each other's style as well as getting on each other's nerves.

All being together is definitely interfering with both wives getting as involved as perhaps they could, for the very simple reason that they are really not vital to the running of the place. Extremely useful yes, certainly, but the milking still gets done, regardless of their presence or absence. And there is really no room for the next generation to become involved at all, except on the very rare occasion, such as in bringing in the cows on a Sunday afternoon when everybody else is off out.

Anyway, that building of our new milking unit is why I have seen quite a lot of plans for same over the past few months. And not one designer gave thought to families who need to look after young children while milking. See how gender correct I am being? And rightly so — I strongly believe that fathers are equally responsible for the care of children.

But can you see any father in Ireland milking the cows while sporting a backpack, or a front pack, bearing a small child? Yet that was one of the suggestions made to me, which mothers could use, if they *had to* milk and mind a child at the same time. (The emphasis is mine.) The underlying implication was, undoubtedly, that milking is man's work, and child-minding women's, and never the twain should meet.

But my son and his wife are working on how the twain shall meet. So I'll keep you posted as, doubtless, Michaella will keep me posted. She is at that delightful age when she tells everything. But, of course, that means I also have to watch what I say in front of her. Those who bring news, take news, we were always warned in my youth....

OCTOBER

Eurotime

How is it that I always see the most interesting bits and pieces of news in the papers only when I am doing the fire? Five minutes is all that job should take, but then something in the newspaper I'm using catches my eye and I am hooked. I just have to read on before I scrunch it up.

Now, of course, I am using up the pile of papers that accumulated over the summer. Eoin is, thank goodness, no longer likely to look for any of those. Woe betide me if I use any recent paper for firelighting. So it was in a paper from last June that I saw the banner headline of 'Farmers will object to Eurotime proposal'.

'Who says?' was my immediate reaction. We are farmers and we certainly would not object. In fact, everybody we talk to hates the clocks going back in October. It really makes the days so short all of a sudden and proves that winter is really upon us once more. Just as it is suddenly spring, when the hour changes in March, and I can get out in the garden again after tea.

That for me is the kernel of the matter. We get up for work at the same time each morning regardless of whether it is bright or not. An extra hour of brightness at the end of the day, however, is an hour of freedom, of choice. So I for one would be all for having our clocks synchronised with Europe. That would allow us to keep our present summertime right through the winter and have double summertime from March to September.

You know, I vaguely remember when we did have double summertime once before — during the Emergency, as the Second World War was known to us all then. Double summertime was then brought in as a daylight-saving exercise, and some of the objections raised against it then are no longer valid nearly fifty years later. It was said then that schoolchildren would be going to school in the dark and that was dangerous, especially on country roads. Why that should be so I cannot fathom because there were no cars on the road anyway during the Emergency.

There are lots of cars on the road now. They are no specific danger to schoolgoing children because I know of no children walking to school, around here anyway. I consider that they are all now spoiled rotten as, winter or summer, they are driven to school and collected again in the afternoons. I never see any more those little bands of children on the roads, such as there used to be, not only in my time but also in that of my sons. Any orchard along the way is now quite safe, as it never was, for generations back. I well remember the excitement of raiding an orchard whose apples were all cookers, even though we had plenty of dessert apples ourselves at home. I daresay my sons weren't innocent either when it came to raiding orchards. My own orchard here was also raided on a few occasions. And I shall spare the blushes of the raiders I recognised — now grown men with families of their own — by not identifying them publicly.

No child, however, has ventured that far for at least a decade. The damsons also now hang, untouched, in rich black clumps on the branches overhanging the roadside ditches. Strictly speaking, these are not damsons but bullaces. They always made sweet eating for us when homeward bound from school. In later years, if I wanted them for jam, I had to gather them, under-ripe, before the national school re-opened again. Otherwise, not one would be left for me.

Now, however, nobody bothers with them — not even myself, since I have so much other fruit already frozen.

Then there was a season for everything and, as children, we knew where to find every fruit and flower in season. Wild strawberries threaded on a stalk of grass could be treasured all the way home. Sour sorrel tasted sweet enough to children unused to sweets. Wood anemones had a similar taste. Blackberries, of course, were devoured, as were haws — welcome when all fruit fails. But we also ate great bunches of the sweet young leaves of the hawthorn in spring before any fruit was ripe, and we sucked the sweetness from each red clover flower found, when homeward bound, and ate the seed-pod fruits of the wild fuchsia.

We weren't always so innocently employed, however. There were regular episodes of 'croosting sods'. I have no idea where that expression came from. But it was a great game for one gang to rush ahead, build up a big pile of grassy sods off a ditch, and then lay in wait behind it to pelt the sods as ammunition at the oncoming group of children. Can't you just imagine the state of us after such a battle royal? Because fresh ammunition was always to hand — as well as the enemy's, which we re-used — it was possible for defenders to turn into attackers and capture both the territory and the stockpile of ammunition.

How clean those little darlings in their cars must stay nowadays! And I notice that a trip to the shop, for sweets or crisps, seems to be normal practice. How they'd turn up their noses at our homegoing treats. I bet, however, that they don't have half the fun. And no extra hour of daylight is going to tempt them to wander the countryside since it appears that watching television is their main occupation when they do get home.

Now, the paper that unleashed all those memories said that it was the Industrial Committee of the IFA who decreed that farmers would prefer things as they are at present. The change would, however, suit businessmen, giving them an

increase in the hours in which they could do business with
mainland Europe. However, '... for the farmers it would
mean an extra hour of darkness in the morning which
would hit production.'

Did you ever hear such nonsense? The corn and the grass
are going to grow at the same rate and get the same amount
of daylight regardless of whether we say it is seven o'clock,
eight o'clock or even nine o'clock. So how on earth could
production be affected? All animals adapt quite happily,
anyway, to whatever routine is set. Think of all those other
countries where milking starts before five in the morning,
every morning.

One student from New Zealand, on leaving, told us that
the biggest difference he found between us here and farmers
in New Zealand was that they get up to milk the cows,
while we seem, instead, to milk the cows when we get up.
And, at that, he wasn't aware that many's the cow in Ireland
that still hasn't even been brought in for milking when we'd
normally be finishing up. Now, for those who like to lie
abed in the mornings, look at all the time they could make
up were we to get that extra hour's daylight. So, perhaps
that extra hour would improve human productivity even if
there is no way it would make a whit of difference to the
productivity of our animals or crops.

Anyway, lets face it. The experts here can pontificate all
they like. It's what England does that will count most. Mark
my words. The status quo will remain until England
changes its time. Then, and only then, will we follow suit.
And what we — or the likes of us — would prefer won't
make one whit of difference to the outcome.

The Test was Clear but the Champers is on Ice

We got a clear herd test last Saturday. And it was a clear clear — no talk of even one doubtful. What a relief that was! If we were champagne drinkers, that would have been the time to crack open a bottle. We didn't, of course. In fact, such a thought never even occurred to any of us, despite our great delight at the news.

'I suppose you opened the champers there and then?' said a fellow farmer and guest at a friend's house the next night. It was said half joking, but wholly in earnest, with a knowing look. All the others present laughed in agreement with him. But, you know, I just stood there, looking at him with my mouth open, and wondering was it the way he isn't living in the real world at all, or is it we who are out of touch? I wouldn't mind the professional or business people. They still have those notions of farmers living the high life.

With us, champagne would have to be brought in specially, and with a celebration in mind. I personally would much prefer to have the price of a good bottle of champagne than the drinking of it. But it is the expected thing to do somehow for births and engagements and, up to this, we have conformed, even if not with Dom Perignon.

The fact that we so easily conform to what is expected is really quite extraordinary when you come to think of it. It shouldn't matter in the slightest what other people say or do. Yet even that stupid kind of implied criticism bothered me that night. It was an occasion for celebration all right, when the test was clear. We were more than delighted after all the worry and stress of these past months. Yet we didn't even stop for as much as a cup of tea in celebration.

There were animals to be taken back to where they had come from for the herd test. The slurry scraping for the day hadn't even been started, the calves needed checking, a cow was just starting to calve — you know yourself how it is.

The work on a farm does not stop just because of a clear test. Yet this man made me feel mean somehow, and, in retrospect, not right in this perfectly normal way of behaving. Then, when the other friends joined in and agreed that we were the hard nuts, and hard on the sons too, I got really uncomfortable and was glad of the first opportunity to change the conversation.

Afterwards, in the car going home, I brought all this up with Eoin. But I got no sympathy or understanding. 'What small things bother you, Liz,' were his exact words. 'Easy known that it isn't they were buying the champagne.'

He dismissed it all so easily. But it was my own reaction in company really that I was dismayed at. That is what conformity is all about. Eoin in the car could be easily dismissive. But if he was actually in that group, on his own at the time, he could not have said it half as easily. Conformity is what we are trained into from when we are children. We must be the same and look the same as everybody else or we feel uncomfortable. If going to a wedding, how quick we are to find out what we are expected to wear, whether it is a dress wedding, and even if it is to be a 'hatty' wedding. Otherwise we feel we stick out like a sore thumb.

Conformity is that wish to be right and to be liked. People really like the company of those who are like themselves, you know. You don't see farmers socialising much with those who genuinely believe that all land should be nationalised, or with people working on the factory floor. Like attracts like. We were mainly farmers that night, all middle-aged, all with grown-up children. So our hard years are over, and that showed. And the principal topics of conversation all night were farming and our children, with occasional excursions into politics and religion. Those are the two subjects people say should be avoided at a dinner party, but how dull life in Ireland would be without them. Yet, how little they matter really is obvious in that nobody cares now whether everybody goes to Mass every Sunday or not, or who we say we are going to vote for at the next election. The norms have changed. This is odd surely. One person that night said that he had not been to Mass for at least ten years, and no notice was taken. But because they thought that we were casual about having a clear test, I was made feel peculiar. When the norm was seemingly established by the agreement that it was the correct thing to celebrate such an occasion with champagne, nobody there challenged that, not even myself. I just kept quiet. But it made me think.

When making decisions we look to people who are like us or, most importantly, whom we wish to be like. We are constantly comparing ourselves to others of the same class as well as to other farmers of like size and sort, to judge how we really are getting on, whether we are doing all right and whether we are right in what we are doing. When things were good in the 1970s there was a lot of social pressure by farmers, on farmers, to be spending money on all the visible trappings of success — new houses, big cars, foreign holidays and the like. Then there was that most obvious success symbol of all — more land.

Everybody seemed to be expanding. Now, while at the time I thought some of the things we saw being done were the height of madness, I must admit that I was also as envious as hell. 'How can they afford these things when they're milking only the same number or even fewer cows than we are?' was what I kept thinking. 'Where are we going wrong?' is the thought that runs through many a person's mind when they see others are doing better than themselves.

The social pressure is on to conform, to be every bit as good. Only a year or so back, nobody would even mention champagne in the context of herd tests. But has the present good prices for milk, beef and calves gone to people's heads? Listen here now, with all those storm clouds on the horizon, I think the farming community had better keep all thoughts of champagne on ice for a good while yet. And anyway, we have another test yet to pass, so what were they going on about?

Don't Call Me Dearie

How I hate to be called 'Dearie'! If one more person had said 'Dearie' to me, I think I'd have exploded, groggy and all as I was after the anaesthetic. I was cross anyway because I was after spending hours on a trolley on a corridor outside the operating theatre for no good purpose that I could see. We are all sick to death hearing about hospital cutbacks and the hardship they are causing. Well I was anyway. But, as the old saying goes, it is easy to sleep on another man's wound. Experiencing these cutbacks personally was quite another matter.

And you know, my trouble was a very small one. I was in hospital only overnight, to have a tooth pulled and a very bad abscess drained. The biggest difficulty was in getting a bed. I had to wait my turn, which is fair enough, and, being sick as a dog with my bad tooth poisoning my whole system, I had no objection when finally offered a bed in a female geriatric ward. This, however, was a salutary lesson to me. Whatever I may say on occasions about feeling absolutely ancient, I now know I am not old at all really. To be really old and ill can be pitiful as I discovered this week. I seriously don't know if I ever want to be that age. But I had better not get into that whole area of living too long because when I jokingly told the family to have me shot if I got too old, Eoin got quite cross with me for talking like that.

My point is something quite different. Why are old women so infantalised by being treated as if they were all helpless children again? All the nurses and young doctors, male and female, as well as the cleaning staff, called every woman in that ward by her first name or, failing that, they used the catch-all phrase 'Dearie'. 'Move over in the bed now, Katie', or 'Time for the bedpan now, Dearie', to respectable women in the ward who I found were addressing each other as Mrs Murphy, Mrs Lynch or whatever. These were women the like of whom we all know, who never call their friends and acquaintances anything except Mrs, no matter if they know them for all of forty or fifty years.

Women, next-door neighbours all their lives, continue to be semi-formal with each other because that is the way they were brought up, and so they are happiest to remain that way. God knows, there are a lot more women I give their full titles to, than women I address by their Christian names. I don't even know the first names of a lot of these women. Yet, once landed into a hospital environment, all and sundry are on first-name basis with them, just as if they were children again.

It is all right for the young. They are much freer in this respect anyway. But why aren't the old allowed their dignity? The rather nasty thought did cross my mind that this is a class phenomenon. Would all these women be Mrs or even Miss Something if they were in up-market hospitals? How are men treated in either place? Is Mr Jack Murphy 'Jack' or is he 'Mr Murphy'? I bet Dr Jack Murphy would never be plain 'Jack', no matter in what hospital he found himself.

Yet it is not as simple as this either, because all the obviously regular visitors to the ward were addressed by the nurses with their full titles. Poor old Mrs Murphy in the bed was Katie, but her sister, by virtue of staying on her feet, was Mrs Kelly. My own personal thoughts on the matter are that once you become a patient in a bed in a hospital, the staff want you to be quiet, uncomplaining, and grateful. Thus the mechanisms of the hospital are geared to childlike helplessness on the part of the patient. And never was that more obvious than in my geriatric ward. It was bad enough to hear them being told what to eat — 'Eat that up now, Dearie, or I'll be quite cross with you' — but when it came to telling them when they needed bedpans, it was a bit much. There were fixed times to relieve themselves — the bedpan round — and all the requests in the world would not get them a bedpan in the off period.

All I could think of was myself telling my children to go to sleep, that they did not want either a drink of water or to go to the toilet. Mother knows best. We all play that game with our children, whether it is with the food to be eaten or the clothes to be worn. I suppose we do this because they are weak and relatively helpless and we need to keep them in control. The same probably applies to the smooth running of the hospitals, but all I know is that I do not want it to happen to me, ever.

Of course, once I was on my feet again, I made enquiries as to why this should be so. One doctor friend of mine said that the nurses get on first-name terms with their old patients so as to make them seem more friendly when they have to do demeaning jobs like cleaning up after them. But he said — and he is a hospital consultant — that it is unforgivable for a doctor to call patients by their Christian names. 'That is interfering with their dignity as a person,' he said, telling me that he is formal even with people he knows, when it is a doctor–patient relationship. If I went to him, in his professional capacity, I would be Mrs Kavanagh and not Liz, even though I've known him since before I was married.

I was strongly tempted then to remark that he was surely distancing himself in order to increase the power and dignity of his position, but I didn't, because I would be arguing against myself and the point I was trying to make. But when I did ask him if he called poor people in public wards by their Christian names, he said he would have to think about that one. He obviously wasn't sure, once I had put the doubt in his mind. That is the trouble with us all. We get so used to doing things a certain way that we are no longer aware of the whys and wherefores.

Take all that time I spent on the trolley in a corridor for instance. I could find neither rhyme nor reason for that. Nobody else got into my bed while I was away. Yet I was almost two hours, bored out of my mind, lying flat on my back in an operating gown, on a trolley, in a public corridor.

They had taken my glasses off me so even if I had had a book, it would have been no use to me. I did ask a passing nurse to get me both from my ward, but of course that was the last I saw of her. And I wasn't even sedated as mine was going to be such a small job. So, I was in the full of my senses lying there.

Only for the fact that my gown did not decently cover me, I'd probably have hopped back to my locker for my book myself. Eoin, who has never in all his life had to undergo any kind of operation, said that if it was him, he'd have been half-way home when they came looking for him, operation gown or not. But he wouldn't of course. Once you find yourself in a hospital situation, you immediately become obedient and childlike and do precisely what you are told. The system works that way. That may be why so many of the things that hospitals do make no sense at all. Anybody who has ever had an appointment for an outpatient clinic for a certain time and then turned up punctually only to find that about another hundred people were given appointments for precisely the same time will know exactly what I mean.

Anyway, the long vigil on the corridor being finally over, I was wheeled in and put to sleep. 'You'll feel nothing when you wake up,' said the surgeon cheeringly, 'because I'll give you a local anaesthetic to take care of the pain for the first few hours, so don't be worrying about that.' Little did he know that at the time I was gone beyond caring what happened. All I wanted was the blessed thing to be gone and finished with. Or so I thought. In actual fact, I woke up in desperate pain. The local anaesthetic just hadn't worked. Sure the reason I was in the hospital in the first place was that my own dentist had failed, because of the deep-seated abscess, to get a local anaesthetic to work well enough for him to yank the offending tooth out. Obviously the same thing had happened again.

Now I knew exactly what it felt like to have a tooth

pulled in past times. It was sheer agony. And I wouldn't mind but the nurse, when I told her this, said nonsense, that couldn't be so — couldn't I see all around me resting quietly? and all those had really big jobs done on impacted teeth; I was in the recovery ward with the rest of that morning's dental operations. She even offered to take me into the next room to show me a young man with his face, top and bottom, on both sides, out to there, and she indicated somewhere six inches on either side of her ears. Then she went off about her business.

Eoin was allowed in then and he wasn't long about changing things. I heard his voice getting cross in the corridor, and next thing the surgeon was in and the nurse was ordered to give me a pain-killing injection. Was it because Eoin was not the patient that he got action, or was it because he is a man? Whichever it was, the relief was just wonderful once the injection started to work and I had no more pain afterwards. But I can still hear that nurse say as she administered it, 'You must have a very low pain threshold, Dearie!'

God but I was cross. I don't ever in my life want to be called dearie again. But how on earth am I to avoid it if I grow too old?

NOVEMBER

More Souls Get to Heaven

This week I got into the jeep to go on a message for the farm and was nearly blasted out of it when I turned on the key to heat up the engine. The radio was turned up to such a volume that it actually hurt me physically. Why on earth do my sons do this? Eoin is forever giving out about it, saying that it has now come to the stage when he first has to turn off the radio before he even dreams of turning a key, no matter what vehicle he gets into. It has become an automatic reflex action with him. And the radio in the milking parlour can be heard half-way across the farm, as well.

'They'll all be stone deaf before they're forty,' says Eoin, ruefully. 'But do you think they'll listen to me? You can't tell these young people anything....'

Yet the odd thing is that I see them all here with their ear-muffs, which they wear whenever they're doing a noisy job. They would not dream of going straw-chopping or working the angle grinder without their ear-muffs on. Yet they must then be undoing all that preventative good with the volume at which they play their 'music'.

And this concern of ours is not just us being fuddy duddy about things. Unfortunately, Eoin knows only too well what life is like if one's hearing goes wrong. He suffers very badly from tinnitus. He has bells ever and always ringing in his ears. Over the years he has been to all sorts of doctors about this complaint, with absolutely no help or comfort at all from any one of them. They have put him on various medications all right — though a drink of cold water would have done just as much good for him. But one thing all the experts did have in common was their opinion that Eoin's hearing was damaged in his youth by noisy machinery.

Tractors, threshing machines, furze-cutters — all sorts of machines were very noisy long ago. Tractors had no cabs to cut down the noise for one thing, and, anyway, young men gloried in the noise they made. They got a grand feeling of power and strength with the roar of their engines. There were no radios to distract them from this satisfaction either. So, what difference did it make if you couldn't hear or be heard over the noise of the tractor engine? The way Eoin tells it, the only thing that could really be heard anyway was the sound of dance music inside your own head, after having been out at a dance half the night before. Then, in exhaustion, he could always rest his head against the mudguard as he drove along, or else the back tyre when he got down, and he would still hear the music of the band playing on and on.

Now all he hears are the bells. 'There must be the world and all of the holy souls calling on me now, to get them out of purgatory,' he said to me, quite matter of factly, one day during the week. For once, I didn't know what on earth he was talking about. I know it's November — the month of the holy souls, and all that. But neither of us is anything like as good as we once were for visiting the graveyard, or a church, and saying the required prayers for the release of the Holy Souls. In fact, we haven't actually done so for many a long day.

So I asked him what on earth the holy souls had to do with anything. I secretly hoped that he wasn't going to go all religious on me in his old age. But it was not a fit of religion was the matter with him. It was just that his tinnitus was particularly noisy and annoying, as it has been ever since his bad fall last summer. Before that he was troubled by only the one ear. Now he complains that both of them never stop ringing, morning, noon, or night.

Eoin told me all that, and then, in genuine bewilderment, asked 'Did they never say to you when you were a child and complained of a ringing in your ear, that that was a holy soul that needed just the one more prayer to get out of purgatory? I was always told then that I was the one chosen to say that prayer. And if I just said, "The Lord have mercy on the dead" the soul would get to heaven and the ringing would go away.'

'And did it?' I asked, ever the sceptic.

'It always did then,' Eoin assured me. 'But devil the bit of good it does me now to say it. It's been that way ever since the powers that be as good as got rid altogether of purgatory. Sure there are either no souls left there now for me to pray for, or else my prayers aren't as good as they used to be when I was a child!'

I was left looking at him in amazement, not because he was deadly serious in what he was saying, but because that was something I had never before heard, in all my years with him. Eoin was quite in earnest telling me of his aunt and the other old people who he'd hear, several times a day, saying, 'The Lord have mercy on the dead'. And one particular aunt used always add on her own little bit: 'And to our own on the Last Day.' 'Whatever that was supposed to mean,' Eoin concluded. But I assume that it was meant as a prayer for the Lord to have mercy on her own soul too on the Last Day.

Now all this was interesting to me because it showed that there must have been a history of tinnitus in Eoin's family and not in mine. Otherwise, why had I never heard in my childhood, nor indeed since, any bell ringing in my ear. Nor had I ever heard that charming, and indeed comforting thought of praying for the dead when you did hear a ringing, and I was brought up in an equally Catholic and rural ethos.

I wonder if, at the time, apart from the religious aspect of the whole thing, it actually helped Eoin — this thinking of others, even those dead, as a distraction from his own personal discomfort. I must remember to ask the boys, sometime, if they ever hear a ringing in their ears as well, since it must be hereditary for them also. I don't fancy my chances, however, even if they do, of getting them to say a prayer for the holy souls.

When his ears are particularly bad, Eoin thinks of those who are gone, but even more so of the young, who just will not be told of the trouble they are undoubtedly bringing on themselves. As he says himself, 'They'll mark my words yet, Liz, when it will be just too late....'

There's nothing whatsoever wrong with my hearing because I cannot begin to tell you quite how often I have heard those exact same words out of Eoin about his sons.

An Elastic Garden

What a magnificent November this has been — a real Indian summer, even if it is a month late. But then again, that has been the story of this year, ever since the spring. You must know that I rarely remark on the weather because, by the time I get into print, things may have changed drastically. So, if there is snow now on the ground, please bear with me. I was so delighted with my day today that I felt I had to write about it.

Today was positively warm and sunny, and all things go better when the sun shines. Our cows are calving away grand and everybody appears to be getting through their work smoothly enough. So, would you believe, today I actually got some help in the garden? I don't know about you, but I find my men-folk here would rather do any work at all in preference to helping in the garden. They are always too busy with something vital when I go abegging. And, if I persist, I am then the world's worst and I hear dark mutterings about how some people just can't seem to get their priorities right — my own words of past years coming back to haunt me.

Actually, however, I am trying to get my priorities right, and the work I wanted done today will save me — if not them — endless effort for all of next year. I wanted the straw from the calving pens brought down to the garden for me — and I was hoping for a strong man to stay and put it exactly where I wanted it, there and then. I know I was pushing it a bit since usually I am considered lucky to have it brought down at all and not just left in a great big dump, somewhere handy to them, but not necessarily for me.

I have been spreading the once-used straw from the calving pens now for years, on the flower borders and in the orchard among all the different kinds of fruit. When you put a good thick layer of straw under the trees and shrubs it acts marvellously as a weed-killing mulch. Nature abhors a vacuum. If the ground is left bare, it will quickly fill with weeds. So, I spread the straw all over the place like a carpet, tucking it carefully around all the perennial plants and under every shrub. The cut-down dahlia plants also get a good lump of straw on top of them, which keeps them quite safe from any frosts. They then grow grand up through it come next spring. So too do the daffodils, tulips and every other bulb or herbaceous plant. It is only the ones that are green now, like the sweet william or pansies, that you have to be careful not to cover. It may look a bit unsightly at first. But I guarantee you that by next spring, when everything is in leaf once more, you'll hardly know the straw is there, except for the absence of weeds. And weeding can be an endless chore, which robs you of the necessary time just to sit and smell the roses.

My garden is, by now, a pretty big one because I never

put a boundary to it. There is no hedge or wall to say, 'This far and no further can my planting go.' So, time after time, I have come around Eoin to move the electric fence paling just another bit out into the adjoining field. Each time he tells me that this is the very last time he's going to move it. I wholeheartedly agree with him, of course, as I help straighten up the new line, even though I may already have future plans floating excitedly around my head. You know the way it is. As you acquire new plants, you just have to have a place to put them, and I never can resist calling in at any garden centre we pass or picking up anything interesting at our country market.

The bigger my garden gets, oddly enough, the easier it seems to be to keep it looking presentable. It's just the same with houses. In a small space everything has to be kept pretty perfectly or it quickly looks untidy in the extreme. In a big garden the larger trees and shrubs give a framework that always looks well, and yet there is enough room to have a good display of whatever is in season at that precise moment.

Personally I think that the secret of appearing to be a really good gardener is to find out what you personally can grow well and easily, and then to grow lots of that. The general effect is everything to the casual viewer. It is only the madly keen gardener who rhapsodises about the unusual — which is usually only unusual because it is so difficult to grow well. Anyway, we all want what we haven't got and forget the value of what we do have. Someone, this autumn, was in raptures here about all my pink hydrangeas, saying that she can grow only the blue ones because of her acid soil. Now I, with my alkaline soil, had gone to considerable trouble to have some blue hydrangeas. These my visitor didn't even notice, so drawn was her eye to what was doing really well.

You know, my kind of garden — the old-fashioned kind of cottage garden — is becoming quite fashionable simply because it is the most showy for the least effort. Going out of fashion is the nurseryman's ideal of shrubs, all of the same variety, planted in multiples. This is doubtless a good idea for immediate effect, if you have the money for it. You do have maximum impact for the short period your one variety is in flower. I get much more value, however, out of the different varieties and the differing seasons of each, plus all the bulbs and herbaceous plants I can manage to squeeze in between. These then support each other, shelter each other, and complement each other in colour or form — except, of course, when I make mistakes like putting pink lupins next to orange oriental poppies, which I have done, with clashing consequences.

The beauty of a garden is ever-changing and nothing need be permanent. Today, for instance, I put the manpower, which I got after dinner, to digging up plants that had become crowded by other choicer specimens. These were then put into that brand-new section, still being planted up since last spring's boundary change. These gave this new area a very mature look, instantly. Having taken it over, I had just sprayed off the grass and covered it with a thick layer of straw. So, it is now in perfect condition for planting, with very little effort on my part.

All in all, I've had a great day in my garden. I picked a big bunch of flowers when my help left me to go to the cows and the winter darkness was fast descending. But it was a bunch of flowers for all four seasons. I picked delphiniums, primroses, roses, and many others which were blooming either too early or too late. What was that prophecy of St Columbanus? — that the end of the world is nigh when you can tell the difference between summer and winter only by the leaves on the trees. Well, that is just how things have been here this week and I have enjoyed every minute of it.

Those Little Mites

There was major commotion here this week. Michaella was sitting on my lap, as she is wont to do while I read to her, when, out of the corner of my eye, something moving caught my attention. No, it wasn't a mouse. It was something even smaller. Missy Michaella had head lice. I still feel my head getting itchy, even telling you about them. But Sara, when she came to collect her daughter, reacted much worse to the news. It was almost as if I was blaming her personally for the head lice on Michaella. God love her. There hasn't been a child ever that did not get head lice at some stage or another in their career. And, as I hastened to reassure Sara, it is the cleanest hair that the lice particularly enjoy.

But that is a hard thing for both parents and children to accept. I discovered head lice on Michaella's father in exactly the same circumstances many years ago. A quick search showed that all five of my sons were infected that same afternoon. I went to the chemist on the spot — never mind the fact that I was due to go milking the cows that evening. Funny, isn't it, the things you remember? As well as the lice-killing lotion, I bought a fine comb. And, because of my bad memories, for the rest of their childhood, I regularly used that fine comb on their heads.

The extraordinary thing is that their head lice always seemed to develop in the autumn months. This is the danger period, as I already knew to my cost. I was sent off to boarding school the September I was thirteen, and to me it was a great adventure. However, a few days after I went there, the whole class had to report to the infirmary immediately after lunch. There we all stood, in line, while this nun took out a fine comb and started to comb through our hair. I took not the slightest bit of notice since my mother had also regularly done that with all my family.

Each girl, as she was finished having her hair examined, was then allowed to leave. My turn came. The nun combed through my hair and, without further comment, told me to stand over there, in front of all the girls remaining. I did not take a lot of notice because at the time the whys and where-fores of that school were a total mystery to me, a newcomer. The only ones who were totally at ease were those who had come up through the prep school and knew the ropes. Those of us who had got our Primary Certs at our local national schools went straight into second year.

Standing apart, I soon noticed that those old hands at the game were sniggering and seemed to be looking pointedly at me. I was the only one standing on my own. And, as girl after girl was left go away, I finished up being the only one in the Infirmary. Then I really got uncomfortable. But that was nothing to what I was soon feeling as the nun took me over to the sink and started in on washing my hair. Then she started asking me questions like whether I had a mother, and finding out that I did, asking me whether she washed my hair, or had I to do it for myself, poor lamb.

Nobody had ever called me a lamb before, not to mind a poor lamb, so I laughed out loud, as much out of nerves as real amusement. Then, when asked why I was laughing, I explained exactly why. This was a very big mistake. The poor nun decided that I was mocking her, got very cross and told me what a dirty little girl I was with nits in my hair and how my mother was a disgrace to have left me come away to a decent school like that!

I can still feel the shock to this day. Nobody had ever in all my life criticised my mother in front of me. It was the most horrendous thing that could have happened. Up to then I really must have believed that my mother was quite incapable of doing anything wrong. Yet here was a nun telling me that my mother was a disgrace and that I should therefore be somehow ashamed of her and for her. It was very confusing for a homesick country girl.

There was further shame waiting for me when I got out to join the rest of my class who were all waiting for me so that we could go for our daily walk. For walks we had to walk in little groups of two, three or four, in front of our accompanying class nun. I had quite enjoyed these walks since the term began, making new friends and staying with the same two girls after our very first day. We seemed to get on fine. But it was not so, this day. I went to join them, as usual, my hair still wet and plastered to my head with vile-smelling lotion, when somebody hissed 'Crawly' at me. Then, with a giggle, those two girls turned their backs on me and joined up with another pair so that I could not tag along. We were strictly forbidden to walk in anything more than fours.

I was left with no choice but to try to tag onto the girls who were walking with the nun. Favourites always got to walk beside her and the misfits fitted themselves in as best they could on the sidelines. And so started my year of misery. The name 'Crawly' stuck for ages, as did the necessity to try to fit in with the misfits on the edges.

Yet I never told my mother the real reason I was so unhappy that first year in boarding school. Somehow I couldn't. After what the nun had said, it would have seemed like a direct criticism, even when I learned that, only a week after I was gone away to school, all the younger family members were found to have head lice too. My mother was afraid of her life I might have them as well, she said to me, years later. 'But, when you said nothing in your letters about that, I knew you had escaped.' And to this day, how I wish I had.

DECEMBER

Gift-giving

For the past ten days the house has been redolent with the smells of Christmas, which waft their way into our section of the building and make me sadly nostalgic. Funny, isn't it, how the sense of smell brings memories to mind, quicker than anything else? That pine smell of a fresh Christmas tree today took me back in memory to when Christmases were Christmases and I, not a daughter-in-law, was the one making the preparations for the festivities.

When they were young my five fine sons never missed the chance of going with their dad to get holly and ivy, and a Christmas tree, from the nearby wood. The last time I walked in that wood I found those lines of trees from which we then helped ourselves still there, and they too are now tall, mature and unreachable.

Yet this has also been my getting-ready-for-Christmas week. This year it is harder work than ever because I am not doing my usual thing of just giving money to all my extended family. Instead, I have gone out and chosen something for each and every one of them. And, what's more, I intend to giftwrap the lot, expensively, sometime between here and Christmas Eve. This is not my style at all. Indeed, I could almost hear my mother's voice echoing at the back of my head, condemning extravagance and mortal sins, as I actually paid out hard cash for two whole rolls of fancy wrapping paper. And what's more, I also paid for a stick-on bow for each and every present I'd planned. As everybody knows, that's not my style at all.

Two things happened this past year, however, to make me change my ways. Firstly, just a few days ago, my little granddaughter, sitting on my lap at her birthday party, when proffered a gift in a supermarket plastic bag, whispered to me privately that it really was not nice when a present wasn't properly wrapped.

I took even more notice, however, of that time earlier in the year when one of my five daughters-in-law was quite cross with me over something trivial. But she hurt me to the quick when she threw in that I evidently thought I could buy people's affections with money. Ouch! Afterwards, she said she was sorry, that she did not mean half the things she said. Taking her literally, my next worry then was which half she did mean. And I determined never again to give that particular family money as presents, just to get my own back if nothing else!

She made me realise, however, when my hurt eased, that gift-giving has a social importance that is usually underestimated. We all know that people say that it isn't the gift that counts but the thought behind it. This is precisely why I think that gift-giving has a symbolic exchange function. A gift is a ritual offering that is the sign of our involvement in, and our connectedness to, another person. And it is characteristic of most supportive rituals that they involve courtesies rather than substantive care. Visiting a sick person is just such a ritual. When you visit, you are not going to do anything really to help, like changing dressings or cleaning the sickroom. Instead, you take a present, which is the ritualised symbol, to show that you care.

Really, the giving of gifts is just one of the means by which we all structure intimate relations with those who are important to us. We give presents to only quite a specific bunch of people. Indeed, it may be quite a useful exercise, at this time of the year, to discover just with whom we exchange gifts. If you do not give people Christmas gifts, no matter how close you think you are, those people are not in your inner ring of intimacy. Or, really to drive home the point, if you do not receive gifts, even though you give them, it means that you are not in their inner circle. Ouch and ouch again.

However, as the mother of sons, very early on in each of their married lives I discovered that Eoin and I stood in line in everything, even in the giving of presents. We were in there, somewhere in that line, behind wife, children, her parents and her close friends. It is easy to understand, however, why this should be so. In gift-giving it is the women who overwhelmingly show that they care. Few of the men I know have given a gift to anybody, except perhaps their wives, in the past twelve months. Indeed, most men have no idea what their wives have given on their joint behalf. And I also bet that few men have taken an active part in any form of gift-wrapping this Christmas.

Now, there's an interesting thing — gift-wrapping. Fancy gift-wrapping is a very modern phenomenon. Long ago, my mother gave a Christmas present of a fine fat goose, to aunts, my priest uncle, the parish priest and various other non-farming friends and relations. Indeed, the delivery of those geese was a big part of the pre-Christmas ritual. But the thought never occurred to my mother to dress them up with red ribbons, or any such nonsense, just to prove that they were presents. Everybody knew that she had reared them from goslings and had also done all the dirty work of preparing them for the table herself. She could hardly have got more personal than that with her presents.

But nowadays, in our capitalist society, the purchase and/or consumption by people of all the things they do not produce themselves has enormous social ramifications, not least in the field of gift-giving. One of the consequences of this situation is that messages of love, sent in the form of

gifts, are in danger of being lost amidst the constant purchase of things in everybody's day to day transactions.
Purchased items, though gifts, no longer stand apart. Thus,
it is the gift-wrapping which serves to bring about a transformation of meaning. Through the act of being covered, the
actual object is made temporarily irrelevant, and the fact
that this object is a gift is made very evident indeed by the
fancy wrapping, bows and such like. However, once the gift
is unwrapped, the object is laid bare once more and must
then take its place among all the other objects in the recipient's possession. So, the act of gift-wrapping is but a temporary solution to the problem of sending lasting messages of
love by means of anonymous, mass-produced objects. Nobody hand-makes things any more.

The problem for gift-giving, in our affluent society, is that
most adults are capable of purchasing, and hence already
possess, most of the things that they really want. So that
makes the ritual of building intimacy by giving presents
more and more difficult.

This is also why, nowadays, over half of the gift objects
given at Christmas are part of a complex gift in which two
or more objects are given to the same person. This is certainly quite true in my case. Buying my presents, I kept
adding in another, and yet another, little thing, especially for
the grandchildren, simply because my original choice did
not seem to be enough somehow.

The rationale behind this doubling and trebling up of our
messages of love is simply to increase the number of signals
in the hope that the repetition of the message will ensure
that it is delivered loud and clear. Giving multiple gifts may
thus be a means of ensuring that a message concerning the
recipient's significance to the donor is received and properly
understood. That goal can also be achieved by repetitive
giving on a variety of occasions.

God be with my courtship days when Eoin regularly
brought a box of Dairymilk chocolates with him when he

came a-calling. In addition, he marked with gifts my birthday, Christmas and also the anniversary of the first day we met. He obviously wanted to make sure his message of love was getting through to me clearly. And I just thought he was a lovely generous man, never realising what was really going on in his subconscious!

But think how disgusted I would have been if he had offered me money instead of chocolates? The abstract nature of money makes it a fundamentally flawed sign of human value. It is usually spent on nothing in particular, and when it's gone, the memory is gone too, as are all traces of the giver. And the personal relationships of family networks depend upon the memory. A good gift, in the sense of love messages, continues to act as a reminder of the giver, at least until the next gift arrives.

Therefore, really good gift-giving entails one or two principal forms. One is a gift of mundane goods — nondurables such as clothes, which are subject to short fashion cycles, and so constantly need renewing. The other, more difficult strategy of good gift-giving is to attune the gift closely to the unique preferences of the individual. Here too clothing is a feasible option since it can be matched both to the individual's needs and taste.

Other successful gifts are the things that the recipient cannot yet afford, or has not thought of acquiring. For example, one of the best Christmas presents I ever got from a son was a small pocket radio, and a battery charger complete with a pack of rechargeable batteries. It was not expensive, about £20 in all. But I have that radio turned on every day since, while I work in the garden. It is marvellous company and never would I have thought of such a thing myself. With the battery recharger I also never run out of batteries. So I am constantly reminded of that son's thoughtfulness in his multiple gift. But that same year I gave all of them money, and that included their wives.

But then again, despite all I've just said, money was all

our sons had ever said they wanted, from their teens on-
ward. And the odd time we gave them a gift instead, there
always seemed to be disappointment in their faces. That is
the problem with giving money — it becomes expected, one
of the perks. There is no continuing message of love behind
it. I also now know, from this year's experience of Christmas
presents, that I have been making a big mistake all those
past years. It is much cheaper to give presents than money.
The sheer bulk of your purchases makes you feel it is
enough that much quicker.

In spite of those angry words during the year, I know
that I never once failed to mark a significant occasion for
those daughters-in-law of mine. Indeed, for each of their
engagements, I parted with a piece of my own jewellery to
mark the event. And I know how to judge whether I am in
or out of favour by whether or not I see those girls wearing
my engagement gift. It is a dead give-away and one I shall
watch with interest after they get this year's presents.

Happy Christmas one and all and I do hope you all get
your messages of love, whether in cash or in kind. And, as
always, it is more blessed to give than to receive. But in the
giving you must always remember to make sure that your
message is received, loud and clear.

The Blessing of ABC Babies

There was a programme on the radio just now with people
ringing in to Gay Byrne about the best Christmas present
they have ever got. They were all material things — from an
engagement ring to a Christmas holiday in the sun. So I
asked Eoin what did he think was his best-ever Christmas
present. Without hesitation, he answered, 'Eoin Óg', which
was just what I was thinking too.

Our youngest son, Eoin Óg, was born on Christmas Eve,

a month premature, another boy after all the others, and an ABC (Absolute Bloody Carelessness) baby at that. He has, however, been our best Christmas present to date. And, whatever about his being an ABC baby, he is the son who is now the most important of all to us because he is the one with whom we share our home and farm.

Every Christmas since, without fail, I recall that Christmas Eve, now thirty-one years ago, when I fought hard against the impending birth, refusing to accept the labour pains as real — I so wanted to be home for Santa Claus coming to all the others. But, as the old people always said, when time comes, child comes, and there is no changing or challenging that.

This is a sad Christmas for us all here this year. I was full of good news to tell of another grandchild on the way. And when could be a more suitable time, in the circumstances, to broadcast the news, than the Christmas issue? But it was not to be. It all went horribly wrong this week and our hearts ache for both Lisa and Eoin Óg, our Christmas baby.

Lisa too fought against accepting the pains she was having for what they were. Hope lives on until quite extinguished. But memories are never fully extinguished. And it was Eoin's memories which came so much to the fore this week, and I learned things I never knew or was just too self-absorbed to understand at the time. Fathers also suffer greatly at times like this.

I may joke about my two youngest children being ABC babies. But, for quite a few years of my marriage, I was certain that I'd never conceive, since nothing was happening. Not that that was a great bother to me if I remember rightly. I just thought myself lucky, those years, when the pill had not yet reached Ireland. But, as time goes on, one changes, and a form of desperation sets in.

So, when I was finally pregnant, although I personally was horribly sick and quite ambivalent about finally getting what we both wanted, Eoin was so ecstatic with happiness that I think, although he made suitable sympathetic noises, he rather enjoyed every manifestation of my pregnancy, no matter how awful it was for me. He even went as far as to get in a store of all sorts of tinned foods lest I express a craving for anything exotic at any odd hour of the day or night. But porridge and cooking apples were my one desire, and the sourer the cooking apples the better. Years later, the local shopkeeper said that she knew each time I was pregnant again because Eoin would start buying cooking apples by the dozen, regardless of the time of the year it was.

Then, one afternoon, just before Christmas, it all went wrong. My mother-in-law tried to prepare me for the inevitable, but I wouldn't believe her. She did the same for Eoin, he now tells me. She also did her best to console him when he left me that night in the hospital when all was over and hope was gone. But, to be quite honest, I was so wrapped up in my own feelings that I didn't really think about what the loss of that grandchild must have meant to her as well. And since she did not live to see even one of her five live grandsons here, that was a loss that was never rectified.

So this Christmas is going to be a quiet one for us all, with all our Christmas memories, both good and bad. With the benefit of hindsight, everything turned out fine in our personal lives afterwards, despite the despair of that time. 'God speaks last,' was a great saying of the old people around here. And when I came home from hospital, that was one of the first things old Maggie said to me. And then she added — in that time of very strong belief in Limbo — that the gates of heaven were open to all anyway, for all the days of Christmas, so that should be a great comfort and consolation to me.

Be that as it may, Maggie then went out of her way to remind me to leave our doors unlocked, that year above all, on Christmas Eve, so that the Holy Family, travelling the earth for a place to lay their heads, could come in to rest awhile, and leave their blessing in the place.

'You'll have a replacement yet some Christmas if you do,' she insisted. 'And be sure to light the Christmas candle yourself this year, and do keep it out of a draught, so that it doesn't blow out at any stage,' she continued. 'Mark my words. That's very important, this year above all, if you are to have good news for us again before long.'

Pure superstition it all was, of course, but these superstitions did give a structure and a sense of meaningful magic to the lives we led. At that time we could 'know' things in a way totally alien to us today when Limbo is definitely and officially gone. However, the significance of the candle not being accidentally extinguished, that year above all others, is still somewhat of a mystery to me. But we did take care, and sure enough, by the following Christmas, Michael, born in October, was bawling lustily in my arms. And five years later my ABC baby arrived early to replace the lost soul that had escaped the Limbo of its time.

When Lisa, now the youngest in this house, lights the Christmas candle on Christmas Eve, I shall remember Maggie with a special private prayer. I will also make sure no draught can come near the candle. And, after they have all gone to bed, I intend to creep downstairs again to undo the locks on at least one of the doors to the house to allow in all good things. I would dearly love history to repeat itself once more, whatever I may just have said about it all being pure superstition.

The Wran, the Wran, the King of all Birds

Not a wren-boy came near us this year — any more than they have done for years past. We, I think, are the poorer for that fact, even if we may have more money in our pockets as a result. The really sad thing for me is that none of my sons, much less their wives, have the least memory of wren-boys ever calling. They know little or nothing of that old tradition. They never had a reason to learn off all the words of the wren-boys either. I did, although as a girl, and a farmer's daughter, it was regarded as none of my business at the time.

The wren-boys were a very important part of the day after Christmas. From early on St Stephen's morning we'd be looking out for them. We'd know they were coming by the singing of their song. I think I remember learning off all the words by listening hard all morning, as group followed group, and then rushing away to write down all I could recall in the middle pages of my school copybook. Well, to be quite honest, I don't remember doing that exactly. I obviously did, however, because there it was, among the memorabilia of me, left by my mother, among her things, when she died. Perhaps it was at national school instead that I garnered the words. But the writing is definitely mine, in still unfaded ink, which belies the date written by me on the top.

I had, of course, an ulterior motive in getting the words of the chant off pat in 1945 when I was nine years old. Before that, I was just a child behind the half-door, half scared and half delighted by the apparitions outside. Depending on the condition they were in, some would be asked to come in and dance for us before being sent on their way. I remember that if that happened, I'd rush behind my mother's skirts. Then I could peep out in safety at the wonder of great big men, all dressed up, with a holly bush bedecked with ribbons, coloured papers, a pig's bladder, and usually several dead birds as well. Now, whether they were wrens or not I have no idea at this stage. But I am positive that they were live dead birds, if you know what I mean. There was usually a drop of bloody mucus dripping from their bills.

When they were gone, my mother would later tell tales of the straw-boys of her youth in her home. She always held that these wren-boys that called here weren't a patch on those she remembered. For one thing, those straw-boys, when they came, were the terror of the young girls, making up rhymes, naming names and suggesting suitable matches for those girls who were of marriageable age but not yet 'fixed up'. We wanted to know if they had ever made up a verse about herself. We weren't told one way or another, but she always had bright pink spots on her cheeks after one of our local wren-boys would whirl her into their dance. My mother was always very light on her feet, be it a waltz or some step dancing.

Then came the St Stephen's Day when my older brother and I decided to go out with the wren ourselves the following year. That was why I had written down all the words so carefully in my copybook. We had the money we were going to get on our rounds well calculated too. If every house was like ours with the money, we'd be in Peggy's legs and blood and bandages for months (for the uninitiated 'blood and bandages' were clove rocks and 'Peggy's leg' was a grand thick creamy-white sugar stick).

When next year came, our scheme was far from forgotten. We spent hours and hours looking for a wren to kill in the days coming up to that Christmas. We had home-made pop-guns with which to do the deed. So, of course, the wrens were quite safe, even if we could have found them. Does anybody else remember those pop-guns, made of one straight, hollow piece of iron tubing, and another solid piece, of equal length, that just fitted inside it? The trick then was to stick the first piece into a raw potato, so that a plug of potato blocked that end. Then, when pointed at the target

and the solid piece forced home, the pressure of air caused
the plug of potato to come out like a bullet of sorts. There
would have been war if we'd thrown stones at each other,
but we were able to do a fair bit of retaliation, legitimately,
with the pop-guns. In fact, we all grew skilled in the use of
pop-guns, straight at the face. A target as small as a wren
was a different matter, however.

So, on that Christmas Day night, I went to bed with ava-
ricious dreams in my head. I couldn't wait to get up and be
off on the St Stephen's morning. My brother, however,
pulled out, for want of a wren, or so he said. But I wasn't
going to let such a little thing stop me. I raided the graveyard in the orchard, where we had laid to rest, with all due
ceremony, various would-be pets that had failed to survive
us. Baby rabbits from our ferreting expeditions and kittens
that fell foul of the dogs were buried there, as was anything
dead we could find when we felt like a good funeral. I knew
we had buried a sparrow just before Christmas — that
would just have to be my wren for the morning. So I turned
grave-robber successfully.

But I did have a real and genuine pig's bladder, given to
me specially by my father, for holding the bucket to catch
the blood during the pig-killing before Christmas. That
year's one wasn't wasted as a football; I carefully saved it
for precisely this occasion by curing it in the smoke up the
kitchen chimney. So that got pride of place on the holly
bush. Then, since my brother would not, I dressed up in his
clothes, had a mask of sorts for my face, and, quite positive I
would pass for a boy, I set out on my own, to call on all the
neighbours. I had already decided that as a money-making
job this just had to beat ferreting for rabbits.

It did. Everyone was most gratifyingly generous. Six-
pences came freely, and there was even one big bright and
shiny half crown. I was on a roll until I made a fatal mistake.
Hubris took over. Now, hubris, of which we have heard quite
a bit lately in political circles, was the pride, or overweening

self-confidence, which led the hero in ancient Greek tragedies to his doom, by making him disregard some fundamen-
tal law. Well, my fatal mistake was to try to see how much
I'd get in my own home. I was absolutely positive I was so
well disguised I'd never be recognised. But I reckoned
without my mother.

A strong arm reached out the back door and pulled me
into the kitchen before I was well into my song. A good
shake detached me from my money. But I did see it again —
briefly. That was when I was made to retrace my footsteps
and return the money to each donor, even that shiny half
crown. No child of theirs was going to disgrace them by
begging, I was told. No matter that at each house they said
that I was well worth what they had given me — I had
danced my one reel and my one jig every time, and had
sung my song in full. Once I had my mind made up to do a
thing I was determined to do it properly, so each household
had had full value for their money. I still handed it back
though. Attempts were made to put some coins quietly back
into my pocket. But, convinced as I was then that my mother
really had an eye at the back of her head, I refused, regretfully.

I think the regrets weren't all on my side though. Why
else did she keep that centre page of my copybook all those
long years? I strongly suspect that their tomboy of a daughter must have caused them great amusement as well as
annoyance all those years ago.

Now here, corrected for punctuation and occasionally for
spelling, is the song of the wren-boys, which I evidently
sang in 1945:

> *The wran, the wran, the king of all birds,*
> *St Stephen's day he was caught in the furze.*
> *From bush to bush and tree to tree*
> *In Tracton's glen we broke his knee.*
> *Although he is little his family's grate,*
> *So rise up good woman and give us a trate.*

Sing holly, sing ivy — sing ivy, sing holly:
A drop just to drink it would drown melancholy.

And if you give us of your best,
I hope in heaven your soul will rest,
But if you give us only small,
Sure it won't agree with us at all.
So up with the kettle and down with the pan:
And give us some money to bury the wran.

Sing holly, sing ivy — sing ivy, sing holly:
A drop just to drink it would drown melancholy.

Give us something new, or something old,
Be it only copper, be it silver or gold
But it's money we want, it's money we crave,
You give us money or we'll bring you to the grave!
Up with the kettle and on with the pan
Give us an answer and let us be gone.

Sing holly, sing ivy — sing ivy, sing holly:
A drop just to drink it would drown melancholy.

So up with the kettle and on with the pan
Give us a penny to bury the wran.
Sing holly, sing ivy — sing ivy, sing holly:
A drop just to drink it would drown melancholy.
So up with the kettle and down with the pot,
Give us our money and let us be off.

Happy New Year, everybody.

EPILOGUE

To Love and to Cherish
— and Manipulate Unnecessarily

This man of mine, like many other Irish 'amadáns', was often fool enough to mention his 'Mammy' to me more than the allotted twice a month. Why do our husbands force us to say those terrible things about their mothers? You know, things like, 'I don't give a hog's a-- how your mother does it' and 'Who gives a hoot what she thinks anyway?', and my own personal favourite: 'Who do you think I am, your mother?' Does it give those Irishmen pleasure to have two women at loggerheads, with them in the middle?

Secretly I think they enjoy it — I really do. And, as for their mothers (poor old gals), they've been giving their sons advice ever since they were little boys, but were made redundant as soon as that ring went on the finger — their jobs having been taken over. It's now someone else's job to tell their son what to do, and this is a privilege that I, like most wives, can't share. Of course 'Can't lives on won't street' as we all know — so okay, I *won't* share.

There I've finally said it.

The moment I met my mother-in-law, she made me feel that I was 'not good enough' for her son. I remember it as if it was yesterday — she all curled up like a teeny-bopper on an over-sized comfortable old armchair in their drawing-room. I liked her honesty and she was able to relax in awkward situations — another wonderful attribute. Once she had educated me to my lowly social status she actually laughed; I mean, she broke into a downright giggle fit. So I thought — a great sense of humour

I was seventeen back then and not fully able to comprehend the whole mother-in-law bit, but if it ever was a subject in which one could receive a university degree, I know that by know I'd have my doctorate. You see, the one thing I could give my husband that his mother could not (or indeed had better not!) was sex — the most powerful tool I knew that would get me the results from my man with raging hormones. And if you are a married woman, you surely know this to be true. So I gathered information wherever I could and made sure I was darned good at it — using one's womanly wile, my husband called it.

I have had a mother-in-law for fifteen years and I still have not gone shopping with her, met her for lunch, indulged in long telephone conversations with her about child rearing, or even had a good auld argument with her. Is this because I took her job all those years ago before she felt she was done? Or maybe she felt that I had that unfair advantage over her son — you know, the one with the raging hormones?

In any case, she raised a wonderful man in my husband for which I am grateful, and I feel she has come to terms with her position in his life. But, to be sure to be sure, I took him 7,000 miles away from her! Now if I could only intercept those e-mails he gets from her, I know I could rest a little easier.

Daughter-in-Law
Summer 1998